Elevate Your Online Store: WordPress & WooCommerce Mastery

Unleash the Power of WordPress and WooCommerce to
Boost Sales and Dominate E-commerce

JOHN L. CODEWELL

Written by:

John L. Codewell

Dedication

This book is dedicated to all who struggle with setup. May it be a source of clarity and guidance, empowering you to overcome obstacles and create the online store of your dreams.

Table of Contents

9. TROUBLESHOOTING AND MAINTENANCE9-107

Introduction

In " Elevate Your Online Store: WordPress & WooCommerce Mastery" we'll dive into the ins and outs of creating a webshop with WordPress and WooCommerce. This book will give you the information and guidance you need to set up a professional and efficient webshop, whether you're a new business owner or an established one wishing to grow your online presence.

Importance of Creating a Webshop with WordPress and WooCommerce

In today's Internet-driven economy, companies of any size need to be visible online. Now more than ever, having a digital storefront is essential for expanding your customer base and bringing in more money, thanks to the rise of online shopping. Your online store may be built and managed with ease using WordPress, a robust and user-friendly content management system, and WooCommerce, a feature-rich e-commerce plugin.

WordPress provides a versatile and adaptable framework for your online store, letting you make a one-of-a-kind shop front that fits in with your brand's aesthetic. Its user-friendly design allows even inexperienced users to quickly learn the ropes and run an effective online store.

However, WooCommerce was developed with the unique needs of an online store in mind. It is fully compatible with WordPress and adds a wealth of e-commerce-specific features and functions. WooCommerce makes it simple to manage inventory, accept payments, keep tabs on orders, and more.

Brief Explanation of Key Concepts and Benefits

In this book, we will explore the fundamentals of building an online store with WordPress and WooCommerce, as well as the many advantages of doing so. Some of the highlights are as follows:

Ease of Use

Both WordPress and WooCommerce aim to make their platforms accessible to users of all skill levels. You will gain an understanding of how to easily create an online store, personalize its look, and keep track of your inventory and orders.

Customization Options

With WordPress, you can choose from a wide variety of themes and plugins to tailor the look and feel of your online store to your customers' preferences. We'll look into various plugins and themes that might improve the functionality and aesthetics of your online store.

Extensive Product Management

WooCommerce offers a full suite of features for handling your store's inventory. Learn to organize your products into categories, define their characteristics, customize their appearance, and maintain an accurate stock level.

Secure and Reliable

When conducting business online, safety must always come first. We'll go through some guidelines for keeping your online store safe, keeping client information private, and preventing fraud.

SEO-Friendly

WordPress is already optimized for search engines, and we'll go over techniques to further boost your online store's rankings. You'll get the lowdown on search engine optimization (SEO) add-ons, keywords, and more.

Analytics and Insights

The success of your online store depends on your ability to analyze and interpret the data. We'll look into analytics programs that can reveal patterns in customer actions, sales figures, and the efficiency of advertising campaigns.

By the book's conclusion, you will know everything you need to know to set up and run a successful online store using WordPress and WooCommerce. This book will serve as a thorough guide to help you build a successful online store and take advantage of the immense prospects given by e-commerce, regardless of your level of experience with these platforms.

1. Getting Started with WordPress

In this chapter, we'll show you how to get WordPress installed and configured for your online store. At the conclusion of this chapter, you will have set up WordPress, selected an appropriate theme, and modified the look and feel of your online store to your liking. You will have the fundamental skills necessary to use WordPress and WooCommerce to build a beautiful and functional online store.

Installing and Setting Up WordPress

To begin installing and setting up WordPress, please follow these simple steps:

Choosing a Hosting Provider

Selecting a trustworthy web host is the initial step in installing WordPress. When you have a website, you need a hosting provider to keep its files safe and available online. Find a service that meets your needs in terms of speed, security, and ease of use in its control panel and customer support.

Registering a Domain Name

WordPress requires a domain name to be registered before it can be installed. Your domain name is the address people will type into their web browsers to visit your online store. Pick a domain name that both describes your company and is easy to remember. It's possible to take care of both your hosting and domain registration with the same company, as many hosting companies also offer domain registration services.

Installing WordPress

WordPress may be installed with a single click through the hosting company's interface. To install WordPress, go to your hosting provider's administrative dashboard. When you select it, the software will walk you through the setup steps. Your domain name, admin user name, and password are required pieces of information.

Accessing the WordPress Dashboard

Once everything is set up, you'll be able to manage your online storefront from the WordPress dashboard. Simply include "/wp-admin" to the end of your webstore's URL (for example, www.yourwebshop.com) to enter the administration panel. To access the control panel, enter the administrator username and password you set up during setup.

Navigating the WordPress Dashboard

Distinct parts of the WordPress dashboard are designed for specific tasks. The dashboard consists of several primary divisions, including the homepage, posts, pages, media, appearance, plugins, and settings. By dedicating some time to exploration, you can learn about the functionality and purpose of each of these components.

Configuring General Settings

You can modify your webstore's default settings in the "Settings" section of the control panel. Everything from the site's name and tagline to the time zone and date format must be specified. Make the necessary changes here to suit your individual tastes and the needs of your online store.

Choosing a Theme

You can customize the look and feel of your online store with WordPress's many available themes. In the "Appearance" tab, you may search for and install both free and paid themes that match the aesthetic and functionality needs of your online store.

Customizing Your Webshop

After settling on a theme, you can tweak it to better fit your company's identity and aesthetic tastes. WordPress's

Customizer is a straightforward interface for changing things like a site's color scheme, fonts, and logo. Learn your way around the Customizer and make tweaks until your online store looks just right.

You can get WordPress installed and ready to go for your online store by following these instructions. You're ready to establish your webstore with WordPress and WooCommerce now that you have a dependable hosting provider, a memorable domain name, and a unique theme.

Choosing a suitable theme for your webshop

Your online shop's aesthetics, features, and user experience will all be affected by the theme you choose. If you want to select the best theme for your online store, do as follows:

Understand Theme Basics

Learning the fundamentals of WordPress themes is a prerequisite to beginning the selection process. Themes are pre-made templates that determine how your online store will look. They control how information is presented and how customers engage with your online store. With so many possibilities available, it's important to find a theme that works with your online store's specific needs.

Define Your Webshop's Requirements

You should first determine the needs and objectives of your web store. Think about things like the goods you sell, your intended clientele, and the feel and image you hope to convey. Which of these styles do you like, or do you want something completely different? If you know what you need, you can start eliminating potential themes.

Research Theme Options

WordPress has a wide variety of options for both free and paid themes. The best place to start looking for a free WordPress theme is the official theme directory. The filters allow you to narrow down the available themes based on factors like popularity, rating, and available options. In addition, look into trustworthy theme marketplaces to get premium themes with cutting-edge features and devoted support.

Consider WooCommerce compatibility

If you're in the process of creating an online store, check to see if any potential themes are compatible with WooCommerce. Try to find WooCommerce-compatible themes or those that are clearly geared toward online sales. The functionalities and aesthetics of these themes are typically designed to work in tandem with WooCommerce to improve the shopper's overall experience.

Evaluate design and layout

The look and feel of your online store should complement your brand and attract customers in your target market. Try to find themes that have fresh, contemporary looks and are easy to navigate. Think about things like the font, color design, and general presentation. Take care with how you organize things like product lists, menus, and spotlights. Remember that a clean, easy-to-navigate design may do wonders for your site's usability.

Check Responsiveness

The use of mobile devices to complete online purchases has made it imperative to select a theme that is responsive and optimized for use on mobile devices. Your online store will look fantastic and perform flawlessly on all types of devices thanks to a responsive theme. View the theme's demo on a variety of devices or use a mobile experience simulator to ensure it adapts to the user's environment.

Read reviews and ratings

You can learn a lot from other people's experiences with a theme by reading their evaluations and ratings before deciding on it. User reviews can be a great resource for learning about a theme's functionality, personalization choices, and developer support. You should give more weight to the higher-rated and positively reviewed themes, as they have a better chance of meeting your needs.

Demo and Preview Themes

Make use of previews and demos to get a feel for a theme's design and functionality before you commit. You may test out the navigation and page transitions, as well as the presentation of your products and other content, in a live demo of a theme. Make sure the interface, navigation, and general user experience are what you'd expect from a high-quality product.

Consider support and updates.

Find out if the theme creator provides dependable support and updates. If you run into trouble or need some assistance tailoring your theme, a developer who has earned your trust will be there to help. The theme is updated on a regular basis to keep it secure and functional with the most recent releases of WordPress and WooCommerce.

Make an informed decision

After doing the necessary research, evaluating the topics, and taking into account the aforementioned considerations, you should be able to narrow your options down to a manageable number. Evaluate the themes in terms of their features, flexibility, pricing (if any), and user reviews. Make a well-informed choice at the end that serves both your webstore's needs and your own.

Keep in mind that a well-designed and fully functional web store hinges on your selection of the appropriate theme. Consider your options carefully, spend as much time as you need researching them, and don't be afraid to ask for help from theme creators or the WordPress community.

Customizing the appearance and layout

The WordPress Customizer is a user-friendly interface for making aesthetic and structural adjustments to your online store. To make your online store just how you want it, follow these simple steps:

Accessing the Customizer

Within your WordPress dashboard, the Customizer may be used by clicking "Appearance" > "Customize." A live preview of your online store will load on the right side of the Customizer window, while settings for those preview changes will appear on the left.

Customizing the Site Identity

You should begin by giving your online store a unique look and feel. Your site's name, slogan, and logo all fall under this category. The "Site Identity" section of the Customizer is where you'll find the options to change these things. Choose a text logo that best symbolizes your company or upload your own logo.

Modifying Colors and Typography

Altering the store's color scheme and fonts might give it a more distinctive appearance. To change the colors and fonts, go to the Customizer's "Colors" and "Typography" tabs. Try out several color palettes and types of fonts until you find one that works for your brand and makes the content easier to read.

Customizing Header and Footer

The header and footer of your online store are crucial in terms of both usability and information display. The Customizer provides settings for adjusting these particulars. You can modify your header anyway you like by including a menu, social media buttons, and a search field. Copyright notices, contact details, and other connections to sections inside the site can all be placed in the footer.

Configuring Homepage Settings

You need to plan out the layout and content for the front page of your web store. The homepage layout choices you have may vary from theme to theme. Find the "Homepage Settings" or "Front Page" option in the Customizer. The homepage can either be a fixed page or a feed of your most recent updates.

Creating Menus

The navigation menus on your website are crucial to the success of your online store. Find the "Menus" tab in the Customizer. You'll find tools to make and modify menu structures here. Make a primary menu for the main navigation and any supplementary menus for the footer or individual categories that you think you might need. You can create new menu items and rearrange existing ones to suit your needs.

Adding Widgets

Widgets let you add more features and material to the sidebar, footer, and other places of your online store that support them. Look for the "Widgets" tab in the Customizer. Discover the various widget regions and drop widgets into them using the drag and drop interface. Widgets are frequently used on websites, and many different kinds exist. Try out a few different widgets to see how they affect the usability and popularity of your online store.

Customizing Page Templates

There are various page templates available for use with some themes, each with its own layout and set of features. A "Page Templates" or "Template Options" tab may appear in the Customizer. Choose a page layout that works for you, such as a full-width design, one with a sidebar, or a landing page layout. You can use the template on as many pages as you like.

Previewing and Saving Changes

The live preview on the right side of the screen is dynamic and reflects any changes you make in the Customizer. Use this function to observe the effects of your alterations on the look of your online store. Click "Save & Publish" once you're happy with the changes to make them available to your webshop's customers.

Iterating and Refining

Keep in mind that tailoring is never finished. It's possible that you'll want to make additional modifications to your online store as time goes on and you gather more consumer feedback. Maintaining an online store's visual attractiveness and usability requires frequent visits to the Customizer.

Changing the look and feel of your WordPress store is as simple as following these instructions and using the Customizer. Take your time experimenting with numerous color schemes, font choices, and layout components to discover the one that best represents your brand and makes shopping there a pleasure for your customers.

2. *Introduction to WooCommerce*

WooCommerce is a robust e-commerce plugin for WordPress, and it will be the focus of this chapter. Thanks to WooCommerce, you can turn your WordPress site into a powerful online store with a wide range of customizable options. We will go over the fundamentals of WooCommerce, such as its features, installation, and critical configurations. After reading this chapter, you will have a firm grasp of WooCommerce's inner workings and be prepared to begin creating your online store.

In this chapter, you will learn the fundamentals of WooCommerce, including how to set up your store and use its most important features. You'll learn everything you need to know to set up WooCommerce for your online store the way you want it. Prepare to use WooCommerce to its fullest extent so you may provide your consumers a fantastic online buying experience.

Understanding the basics of WooCommerce

WooCommerce is a robust e-commerce plugin that works in tandem with WordPress to simplify the process of setting up and running an online business. First, let's have a look at the fundamentals of WooCommerce:

What is WooCommerce?

WooCommerce was created as a free, open-source add-on for online stores. It's a plugin that extends the capabilities of your WordPress site so you can run an online store, complete with product listings, order management, and payment processing. With WooCommerce, you can tailor your online store to meet the unique requirements of your company.

Features and Benefits

WooCommerce's abundant features make it a great option for developing an online store:

Product Management

WooCommerce has a simple interface that makes it easy to manage your store's inventory. You may make new categories, add attributes, specify prices, handle stock, and display product descriptions and pictures.

Payment Gateways

WooCommerce is compatible with numerous credit card processors, PayPal, and other payment gateways. Provide your consumers with easy-to-use payment options by taking advantage of this.

Shipping Options

Shipping methods can be customized, shipping zones established, and shipping charges determined according to parameters such as package weight, final delivery address, and order total. This will guarantee your customers' packages are delivered quickly and accurately.

Customization

WooCommerce provides a great deal of flexibility thanks to its wide variety of available themes and extensions. You have complete control over the look and feel, as well as the features, of your online store.

Analytics and Reporting

WooCommerce's in-built analytics tools let you keep tabs on business operations and learn more about your customers' buying habits. You may then use this information to make educated decisions about how to best run your store.

Integrations and Extensions

WooCommerce can work with many different services and plugins because to its smooth integration with them. Your webstore will benefit greatly from incorporating third-party apps like CRM and email marketing platforms.

WooCommerce is a popular e-commerce platform because it supports a wide range of extensions that can be used to extend its core functionality and add new features like subscription management, complex product variants, and support for multiple vendors.

User-Friendly Interface

WooCommerce is built from the ground up to be simple to use. Because of its user-friendly design, it can be used by those with a wide range of technical knowledge. While the admin panel is where all the action happens, the frontend is where your clients will experience a streamlined buying process.

Community and Support

There is a large and helpful community of WooCommerce users, including programmers, designers, and business owners, who work together to improve and maintain the platform. Extensive documentation, forums, and tutorials are available to assist you in solving problems, learning new skills, and keeping abreast of the newest WooCommerce developments.

Scalability and Growth

As your company grows, so can your WooCommerce-powered online store. WooCommerce is scalable and can keep up with the needs of your business as it grows, whether it's a one-person operation or a multinational conglomerate.

As your company expands, you can quickly add more goods, expand your server capacity, and add new features.

WooCommerce is a robust plugin for the WordPress e-commerce platform that makes it easy to create and run an online store. It's a great option for organizations of all sizes thanks to its numerous features, adaptability, and user-friendly layout. WooCommerce provides the framework for a profitable online store, complete with all the necessary tools.

Installing and configuring the WooCommerce plugin

When combined with WordPress, WooCommerce's robust e-commerce features can turn any website into a fully-featured online store. Let's take a look at the procedure in detail:

Getting Ready for Setup

Make sure your WordPress site is up to snuff with the prerequisites before installing WooCommerce. An up-to-date version of WordPress, a compatible hosting environment, and a self-hosted WordPress site (not WordPress.com) are all necessities. Make sure you have a recent copy of your website's files and database, and that you can log into the WordPress dashboard as an administrator.

The WooCommerce Plugin Setup

Here's how to set up the WooCommerce add-on on your site:

- Go to your WordPress control panel and look for the "Plugins" menu item on the left.
- To browse available WordPress plugins, select "Add New" from the WordPress menu bar.
- Enter "WooCommerce" into the search box and try again.
- If you're using WooCommerce, you can find the plugin in your search results and then select "Install Now."
- When the plugin installation is complete, you may activate it by clicking the "Activate" button.

Initial Configuration Wizard

Once WooCommerce is activated, a configuration wizard will appear to walk you through the basic set up. Your store's location, currency, payment methods, and shipping options are just some of the fundamentals that the wizard will help you set up. Simply respond truthfully to each request and then click "Continue" to move forward with the process.

Store Location and Currency

Give details about your store's location and the cash it will accept. WooCommerce needs this details to figure out what to charge for taxes and shipping. Make sure the country and currency you select fits in with how your company operates.

Payment Methods

Pick which payment options you'll accept from your clients. WooCommerce supports a wide variety of payment methods, such as PayPal, Stripe, and even cash on delivery. Consider your intended clientele and business needs when deciding on a payment option. Set up each form of payment by entering your account information or API keys.

Shipping Options

Adjust your delivery options as needed for your online shop's shipping strategy. Pick a shipment model, such as a flat rate, free shipping, or real-time shipping costs. Establish shipping zones, naming the regions within them and detailing the shipping options and costs for each zone.

Recommended Plugins and Store Enhancements

WooCommerce may suggest plugins or extensions to further expand the capabilities of your online shop. Features like enhanced search engine optimization (SEO), social media integration (SI), and sophisticated product customizations can all be added with the help of suitable plugins. Check out the suggestions and pick the add-ons that work with your company's strategy. Set them up and adjust their settings as instructed.

Store Appearance and Design

Choose a theme that works with WooCommerce to change the look of your online shop. There is a large variety of both free and paid themes available, all of which have been developed with WooCommerce in mind. To check out all of WordPress's theme options, go to the dashboard and select "Appearance" > "Themes" > "Add New." Simply download, install, and activate your chosen theme, and then tweak it to your liking via the theme's settings and options.

Essential WooCommerce Settings

Once you've finished the first setup procedure, you can go into the WooCommerce settings and really make your business your own. Select "WooCommerce" > "Settings" in the WordPress admin menu. General store settings, product settings, tax settings, shipping settings, and more can all be adjusted in this section of the admin dashboard. Examine and modify each option in light of your unique business needs.

Testing and Launching Your Store

Be sure to give your online shop a good workout before opening to the public. Start with a small test order to make sure everything goes smoothly throughout the full rollout. Check that clients are receiving order confirmation emails, that taxes and shipping costs are being calculated appropriately, and that payment mechanisms are working properly.

After you've finished the testing phase and are confident with the store's performance, you may open it to the public and begin selling your wares.

The WooCommerce plugin for WordPress makes it easy to turn your site into a fully-functional store, with only a few clicks of the mouse. If you follow these instructions, you'll have a much easier time getting your online store up and running and ready for business.

Exploring the essential settings

WooCommerce's flexible settings give you the freedom to create a storefront that perfectly suits your company's demands. Now, for the meat of the matter:

General Settings

WooCommerce's General Settings page is where you'll find the most important customization settings for the store's functionality and look. Location, currency, and measurement options, as well as how prices are displayed, can all be customized here. The default customer address, product ratings, and inventory management parameters can also be altered.

Product Settings

The Product Settings section is where you'll handle how your products are shown to customers. You can choose to enable reviews and ratings, define default product dimensions, and organize and categorize your products anyway you see fit. Setting low stock thresholds and enabling stock management notifications are two examples of the inventory management choices available here.

Tax Settings

Accurately configuring tax settings is critical for legality and efficient running. You can establish tax rates for various jurisdictions, tax calculation techniques, and tax classes in the Tax Settings tab. WooCommerce gives you options for dealing with taxes, so you can set up tax-inclusive or tax-exclusive pricing as needed for your region.

Shipping Settings

In the store's admin panel, you'll find the Shipping Settings tab, where you can adjust several shipping-related settings. You can create delivery methods like flat-rate or table-rate shipping, and determine shipping rates based on criteria like weight or order total. Handling fees, free shipment, and integration with third-party shipping providers can all be set here.

Payment Gateways

You can set up the various payment gateways that will be available to your clients. In addition to online choices like PayPal and Stripe, WooCommerce also offers bank transfers and other offline payment methods. Depending on your preferences and the needs of your intended audience, you can enable or disable certain features that come standard with each payment gateway.

Account and Privacy Settings

Under the Account and Privacy Settings button, you can choose how your shop deals with client accounts. You have the option of allowing consumers to check out as "guests" or forcing them to sign up for accounts. Data retention and privacy restrictions, such as General Data Protection Regulation (GDPR), can also be configured via the privacy policy pages you designate.

Emails Settings

You may modify who receives emails and what they say in the Emails Settings tab. Email templates can be customized for use in response to specific events, such as the receipt of an order, the dispatch of an order, or the cancellation of an order. Add your store's logo and contact information to these emails, and make sure your customers understand everything you're telling them.

Integration Settings

WooCommerce is compatible with a wide range of third-party services and platforms, and the Integration Settings tab allows you to set up connections between your store and these additional resources. Google Analytics, Facebook, and MailChimp are just a few examples of the many services with which you can set up an integration. You can streamline your marketing efforts, monitor website traffic, and handle social media campaigns with the help of these connectors.

Additional Settings

WooCommerce gives you the freedom to tailor your online shop exactly how you want it. You have the option of enabling or disabling consumer reviews, as well as selecting your own criteria for reviewing products. The look of the shop can be adjusted in a number of ways: by changing the archive pages, making new endpoints, and adjusting the dimensions of images.

Extensions and Add-Ons

The functionality of WooCommerce can be further enhanced by installing one of the many available plugins and extensions. You may improve your store's security, accept more payment types, offer more shipping methods, and customize your products with the help of these add-ons. Discover the many extensions and add-ons available to expand your store's functionality by browsing the

WooCommerce marketplace or the websites of third-party developers.

You can fine-tune your online shop's performance, customer service, and overall experience by digging into WooCommerce's configuration options. Review all of the options and think about how they relate to your needs and preferences before making any changes. You can make your online shop stand out from the crowd with the help of WooCommerce's adaptability and personalization features.

3. Setting Up Your Product Catalog

In this section, you'll learn how to configure your WooCommerce store's product catalog. In order to draw in customers, showcase your products convincingly, and increase sales, you need a product catalog that is both well-organized and comprehensive. We'll show you how to set up product categories and attributes, add and edit products, and make the most of product tags.

When you're done with this chapter, you'll know everything you need to know to manage your WooCommerce product catalog effectively. Customers will be able to browse your store with ease, locate the products they need, and make educated purchases if you take this step. Let's go in and get started creating that killer WooCommerce product catalog.

Creating product categories and attributes

The easier it is for customers to browse your store and locate what they're looking for, the more time they'll spend there.

Let's have a look at the process of developing product groups and attributes:

Understanding Product Categories

The categories you create for your products will create a natural hierarchy. They aid clients in navigating your store with ease. Identify the characteristics of your products and decide how you'd want to organize them before making categories. If you run a clothes store, you could divide your products into sections labeled "Men's Clothing," "Women's Clothing," "Accessories," and so on.

Creating Product Categories

Here's how to set up product groups in WooCommerce:

- Enter your username and password for your WordPress admin area, then click to "Products" > "Categories."
- Select the "Add New Category" tab.
- Type in the category's name and, optionally, a slug (a shorthand form of the term for use in URLs).
- Creating a tree-like structure is possible by designating a parent category.
- You can provide extra context for the category by writing a short description.
- Click "Add New Category" to save the new group.

This process should be repeated for each new group you want to make. Categories can be added, removed, or changed at a later date.

Understanding Product Attributes

Attributes for products are extra information about those products. You can use them to make new variants of a product or to select products that meet certain criteria. If you're selling t-shirts, for instance, you could use variables like "Size" and "Color" to provide buyers a range of customization possibilities.

Creating Product Attributes

Here's how to add properties to your products in WooCommerce:

- Access "Products" > "Attributes" in the WordPress admin menu.
- Specific attributes can be named with "Color" or "Size."
- Pick whether the property is used for filtering products or allowing for variances.
- Based on the nature of the attribute, choose the attribute type (such as text, select, or color).
- Type in the values for the attributes, such as "Red," "Blue," or "Small," and separate them with the pipe (|) symbol.

- Click "Add Attribute" to permanently store the attribute.

For each new attribute you wish to create, follow these instructions again.

Assigning Categories and Attributes to Products

You can begin classifying and labeling your products once you've established your categories and qualities. You can choose the appropriate category and attribute values for a product as you add or modify it. Products can be more easily found and filtered through the catalog if they are given the proper categories and attributes.

WooCommerce allows you to properly manage your product catalog by setting product categories and attributes, which improves the browsing experience for your customers. Spend some time thinking through the best way to organize your categories and attributes so that your site is easy to use. If your online store's catalog is well-organized, clients will have an easier time browsing and purchasing items.

Adding and managing products

One of the first things you should do when opening an online shop is to start adding products to it. To guarantee that you have a thorough understanding of adding and managing your products in WooCommerce, we will go through everything from product information to inventory management.

Adding a New Product

Add a new item to your WooCommerce store by doing the following:

- To add a new product, go to your WordPress admin area and click "Products" > "Add New."
- Please provide your product with a title. It is customary to use the name of the item being sold here.
- Fill out the main text field with a thorough explanation of the product. Describe the product's advantages, features, and technical details.
- Fill out the "Regular Price" area with the product's pricing. The "Sale Price" section is where you should put the discounted price if the item is currently on sale.
- Put the item into a preexisting category, or several. This makes it much simpler for potential buyers to peruse your collection.
- If necessary, add tags to the products. Tags are product-descriptive keywords that can be utilized in a search engine's keyword filter.

- Choose a hero image that best illustrates the product. You can use this picture in your catalog and detail pages.
- Stock Keeping Unit (SKU), Product Type (simple, variable, grouped, etc.), and Product measurements (weight, measurements, etc.) must all be set up.
- Select the preexisting attribute values for any more product attributes you'd like to add, including color, size, or material.
- If your product comes in different sizes or colors, etc., you'll need to set up product variations. Include details such as pricing, available stock, and photos for each variant.
- To sell a digital file, check the "Virtual" box and add the file to the "Downloadable Files" area.
- Click "Publish" to save your work in progress.

Managing Products

After you've uploaded products to your WooCommerce store, it's time to get them under control. Some fundamentals of product management are as follows:

Editing Products

Go to "Products" in your WordPress dashboard and then choose the product you wish to modify. Make the required changes, then hit "Update" to commit them.

Inventory Management

WooCommerce has tools for handling stock levels. To guarantee you have up-to-date inventory data, you can set stock quantities, enable or disable stock management, and set up low stock warnings.

Stock Status and Visibility

Product availability and display can be managed by you. Pick a stock status: "in," "out," or "backorder." In addition, you can regulate your product's exposure in search results and on category pages by adjusting its visibility setting.

Product Images

Including many photographs of a product increases its attractiveness to the eye. Present the product in a variety of close-ups, medium-range images, and long-range landscapes. The product gallery allows you to post and manage photographs.

Product Reviews

Turn on/off the ability for customers to rate and review products. Reviews have the potential to serve as social evidence before making a purchase. Having customers rate and review your products helps establish their reliability.

Product Attributes and Variations

The product editing screen is where you'll go to make any changes to the product itself or any of its variations. Do what needs doing, like adjusting the prices for the variations or adding new attribute values, and then save your modifications.

Bulk Actions

Products can have their prices, stock levels, and categories changed en masse in WooCommerce. When updating numerous items concurrently, this comes in quite handy.

Product Duplication

Time can be saved by replicating a product if many goods share identical characteristics or configurations. This will make a copy of the product with the same parameters so you can tweak it to your liking.

You may create a thorough and well-organized product catalog by adding and managing your products efficiently with WooCommerce. Maintaining an up-to-date catalog requires regular attention to details like product descriptions, stock levels, and prices. Effective product management allows you to streamline your consumers' shopping experiences and increase your revenue.

Utilizing product tags for organization

You can improve your online shop's usability by using "product tags," which are essentially keywords or labels you apply to your products. Strategic product tagging can improve your clients' time spent shopping on your site and make it easier for them to locate the goods they're looking for. We'll get into the specifics of how to use product tags in just a moment.

Understanding the Purpose of Product Tags

Tags on products are labels that describe them and allow for easier categorization and grouping according to shared features. In addition to standard product categories, they add a deeper level of classification for more refined searching and sifting. If you're in the clothing business, for instance, you could use categories like "summer collection," "formal wear," and "casual attire" to categorize your products and make them easier to search.

Creating Relevant Product Tags

Product names and descriptions work best when they reflect the product's most salient features and qualities. Try to anticipate the terms that potential buyers could use in a search engine. Make labels that are clear, specific, and succinct. Don't use words that could be misunderstood by your customers. Use tags that fairly and accurately describe the product or its intended purpose.

Assigning Product Tags

Here are the steps you need to take in order to tag your products in WooCommerce:

- Go to "Products" > "Add New" or choose an existing product and click "Edit" to make changes to it in your WordPress dashboard.
- Find the "Product Tags" area in the product editing screen.
- Separate the tags with commas and enter them into the text field.
- WooCommerce will autocomplete tags as you type if they already exist. d. Tags already in use can be selected and used to label the goods.
- If you insert new tags that don't already exist, WooCommerce will make them for you. e.
- Think about including numerous tags for each product to increase discoverability and expand search options.

Organizing and Filtering Products with Tags

After tags have been applied to products, shoppers can use them to conduct more refined searches. WooCommerce offers several ways for shoppers to look for products using tags:

Search With Tags

You should add a search bar to your online shop so that customers may hunt for specific labels. If users type in a keyword, WooCommerce will return results for that keyword.

Navigation Through Tags

When customers see a tag on a product page or in a list of products, they may click on it to see all products that have that tag. This opens the door for them to check out related products you sell.

Tag Clouds

A tag cloud is a visual representation of the most popular and often used tags in your store, and it is an option provided by WooCommerce. In the cloud, customers can browse products by clicking on tags.

Navigation Using Widgets

Tag widgets can be placed in your shop's sidebar or footer to facilitate tag-based browsing. These widgets can be modified to reflect the aesthetic of your shop.

Tag Management

Keep your product descriptions up-to-date and well-managed by reviewing and editing them on a regular basis. To ensure uniformity, please remove any tags that are no longer relevant or merge any tags that are too similar. Managing your tag system is a breeze with WooCommerce because you can do so right from the WordPress administration panel.

If you use WooCommerce product tags correctly, you can help your consumers find what they're looking for more easily and expand your store's organizational structure. Improve the user experience, shorten the buying process, and boost conversion rates through strategic tagging. Spend some effort developing tags that accurately describe the content they accompany, and test and tweak your tagging system on a regular basis to make sure it serves your consumers.

4. *Managing Orders and Customers*

In this chapter, we'll look at the nuts and bolts of your WooCommerce store's order and customer management. The success of an online store depends on your ability to efficiently process orders, accept payments, and assist customers. We'll go into common scenarios like refunds, returns, and exchanges as we discuss order processing, payment processing, customer information management, and more. Mastering these areas will allow you to give your customers a positive shopping experience and solidify your connection with them.

Reliability, trustworthiness, and outstanding customer service are the cornerstones of a successful online business, and you can achieve all three with careful order and client management in your WooCommerce site. A pleasant customer experience can result in enhanced customer loyalty and business expansion if the transaction is processed quickly, payments are processed securely, customers are kept informed, and returns and refunds are handled expertly. Let's go into the depths of order and customer management to improve your online store's efficiency.

Processing orders and handling payments

Here, we'll dive into how to process orders and payments quickly and easily on your WooCommerce store. Streamlining these processes is essential for the success of your e-commerce firm and the satisfaction of your customers. Come with me as I get into the details of taking money and fulfilling orders:

Order Notification and Management

Having a system in place to receive and manage order notifications is crucial when customers place orders in your WooCommerce business. WooCommerce's order notification features include email alerts, dashboards for tracking orders, and connections to external services. Modify your alert settings to get real-time updates anytime an order is placed.

Order Fulfillment Process

When an order comes in, it needs to be processed immediately. To process orders quickly and easily, do as follows:

Review the order details
Check the products, quantities, and any special instructions the customer may have provided with the order.

Prepare the order for shipment

Protect the goods during transport by wrapping them in sturdy packaging. Don't forget to include any advertising materials or supporting paperwork.

Generate an invoice

Make an invoice that details the order's products, pricing, and any taxes or discounts. The client may be mailed this invoice for record-keeping purposes.

Mark the order as shipped

Make sure you change the order status in WooCommerce to "Shipped" once the package has left your facility. If it is possible to do so, please provide the customer with tracking details so they know how their shipment is doing.

Payment Processing

For an online store to succeed, it must be able to process payments quickly and easily. WooCommerce is compatible with a wide range of payment gateways, credit card processors, and even cash-on-delivery services. These principles will help you process payments safely and reliably:

Enable secure payment gateways

Install protected payment processors like PayPal, Stripe, or others. Set up your API credentials or bank account information to make financial dealings a breeze.

Test payment functionality

Before opening for business, run test purchases using a variety of payment options to make sure everything is in working order. This will allow you to spot problems ahead of time and fix them before they affect sales.

Monitor payment status

Verify that all orders are being paid for promptly. Make sure all payments go through, and keep tabs on any that don't. WooCommerce's order management dashboard gives you an easy-to-understand snapshot of your customers' current payment situations.

Handle payment disputes

There may be times when customers express dissatisfaction or file a dispute regarding a charge. Respond quickly to the customer's inquiries about payments by maintaining open lines of communication. Strive for a mutually agreeable solution within the bounds of your store's standards and the requirements of your payment processor.

Order Tracking and Customer Notifications

Customers like it when you keep them updated on the status of their orders. Keep customers up to date with the help of order tracking and alerts:

Order tracking

If it makes sense for your business, include an order tracking feature. Customers can check on the whereabouts of their packages using your website or a third-party service.

Order confirmation emails

Immediately after a consumer places an order, you should send them a confirmation email. The purchase summary, shipment address, expected delivery dates, and your contact information are all crucial pieces of information to include.

Shipment notifications

Notify customers of shipment status and expected delivery date once orders have been shipped. This improves communication and openness with the customer throughout the entire delivery process.

Your consumers will have peace of mind knowing that their orders will be processed quickly and securely through your WooCommerce business. Customer happiness and the continued success of your e-commerce venture are reliant on your ability to implement efficient order management procedures, safe payment processing, and clear lines of communication.

Understanding customer management and communication

The best way to increase client loyalty, sales, and goodwill is to develop meaningful connections with them. You may give excellent service and make your customers feel valued by learning the fundamentals of customer management and employing proactive methods of communication. Let's get into the details of client relations:

Collecting and Storing Customer Information

Securely collecting and storing client data is vital for efficient management. Information collected from customers in WooCommerce includes their names, email addresses, billing and shipping addresses, and a record of their purchases. Implement sufficient safeguards to protect client data and ensure compliance with privacy laws.

Creating a Customer Database

Customers' interactions, purchasing histories, and preferences may all be easily tracked with a single database. WooCommerce has in-built tools for managing customer data. Using these resources, you may look up specific customers, examine their order histories, and learn more about their shopping habits. This data can be used for a variety of purposes, including more precise advertising, more relevant promotions, and more specific assistance for customers.

Delivering Excellent Customer Service

E-commerce success is predicated on providing exceptional customer care. Always go the extra mile to satisfy your customers and aid them in every way you can. Key strategies to providing outstanding customer service include the following:

Prompt and Responsive Communication

Get back to customers as soon as possible after they contact you. Clearly communicate expected response times and act quickly to resolve client concerns.

Personalized Interactions

Customers appreciate it when businesses show them special attention by using their names. Put your research to use by personalizing your comments and suggestions.

Clear and Concise Communication

Use simple language while interacting with customers. Don't use complicated or technical language. If detailed instructions are required to help a consumer, please provide them.

Active Listening

Pay close attention to what the client is saying and asking. Exhibit compassion and sympathy. Restate their worries to double-check that you have comprehended their requirements.

Problem Resolution

Make an effort to quickly and effectively fix problems when they arise for customers. Determine the nature of the issue and offer a solution fitting that description, such as a replacement, refund, or shop credit.

Utilizing Customer Feedback

Your products, services, and overall customer experience can all benefit from hearing from your customers. Use surveys, evaluations, and follow-up emails to solicit comments from your clientele. Look at the comments people have left to see where you might make improvements to better serve your customers.

Proactive Communication

Customer relationships can be strengthened and engagement levels increased through proactive communication. Think about using the following methods of interaction:

Order Status Updates

Keep consumers up-to-date on the progress of their orders. Maintain communication with them throughout the order's processing, shipping, and any delays that may occur.

Personalized Recommendations

Make use of client preferences and past purchases to tailor product suggestions and special offers to each individual.

Marketing and Promotional Emails

Offer discounts, make notifications about new products, and promote seasonal sales by emailing your customers directly. Personalize these messages for each individual consumer.

Abandoned Cart Recovery

Send abandoned cart emails to customers automatically to encourage them to finish their purchases. Give them a reason to come back and finish their business with you by giving them a discount or other incentive.

Loyalty Programs and Rewards

Use customer loyalty programs to thank loyal consumers and increase repeat purchases. Provide your most loyal consumers with preferential pricing, advanced previews of new offerings, and other benefits.

Your WooCommerce store's success depends on your ability to handle and communicate with your customers effectively. E-commerce businesses succeed in the long run when they provide a satisfying shopping experience for their customers through proactive customer service techniques, the use of client feedback, and open lines of communication.

Dealing with refunds, returns, and exchanges

In the pursuit of customer delight, it's prudent to have a plan in place for dealing with returns, exchanges, and refunds. To properly manage customer problems and preserve strong connections, one must be familiar with the best techniques for handling such situations. The specifics of dealing with returns, refunds, and exchanges will be discussed below.

Establishing Refund and Return Policies

It is important to lay out your store's refund and return procedures in detail before tackling individual issues. Refund and return policies spell out the procedure that should be followed by customers if they choose to make such a request. Think about things like refund/return deadlines, valid justifications, and product condition/packaging criteria. Put up a page on your site just for refunds and returns, or include the information in your terms and conditions.

Handling Refund Requests

It's crucial to respond quickly and politely to refund requests from customers. To efficiently handle requests for refunds, consider the following:

Understand the Reason

Talk to the consumer and find out why they want a refund. Find out if the request fits the criteria of your refund policy.

Assess Eligibility

You can tell if a consumer is entitled to a refund by looking at their purchase history, order data, and whether or not they followed your return policy. Think on things like how long it's been since you bought the item and how well it's held up.

Communication and Resolution

Give the customer an answer that is both informative and sympathetic. Offer a range of resolutions, including cash back, store credit, and replacement items. Strive for a solution that satisfies both the customer and the store's policies.

Process the Refund

As soon as the return is accepted, you should start the refund procedure. Refunds can be processed either automatically through the payment gateway or manually by following the instructions provided by the respective payment processor.

Update the Customer

Make contact with the client to let them know that the refund has been made. Please submit any supporting materials or information required for the return.

Managing Returns and Exchanges

Customer dissatisfaction or the necessity to switch to a new size, color, or model are two common reasons for product returns and exchanges. These recommendations can help you handle returns and exchanges efficiently:

Understand the Reason

Get in touch with the consumer and find out why they want to send an item back or exchange it. Find out if the customer's situation fits under your return policy and if they are qualified for a refund or exchange.

Provide Instructions

Make sure the customer understands what they need to do to return or exchange an item. Include instructions for proper packaging, return mailing labels, and any other necessary paperwork.

Process the Return or Exchange

Quickly process the return or exchange after receiving and inspecting the returned merchandise. If a replacement is needed, it must be sent out as soon as possible.

Communication and Resolution

Maintain open communication with the customer all through the refund or exchange procedure. In addition to answering their queries, keep them updated on the progress of their request.

Update Inventory

If a product is returned or exchanged, it must be reflected in the inventory system. In this way, you won't have to worry about overselling or catalog inaccuracies.

Continuous Improvement

It's important to routinely analyze return, refund, and exchange data for any discernible tendencies. Examine the causes of complaints or product problems in order to fix them. Think about things like product quality, packaging, correct sizing, and the ease with which products are described. Make use of this information to enhance future product offerings and reduce the need for returns, exchanges, and refunds.

You can show that you care about your customers and keep a good relationship with them by handling returns, refunds, and exchanges efficiently in your WooCommerce store. You can confidently handle these situations and convert them into opportunities to increase customer loyalty and trust by setting clear policies, communicating immediately and effectively, and consistently upgrading products and procedures.

5. *Enhancing Your Webshop's Functionality*

Several methods for improving your WooCommerce-based online store's performance are discussed in this chapter. While WooCommerce is a great starting point for an online shop, it can be customized to better serve your company's needs and offer a one-of-a-kind experience to your customers. Here, we'll explore the various options for enhancing WooCommerce's functionality by adding plugins and extensions, integrating new payment methods, and employing premium WooCommerce themes. You may differentiate your webstore from the crowd in the cutthroat world of online shopping by implementing these upgrades.

Create a one-of-a-kind and feature-rich online shop that stands out from the competition by extending the functionality of your webshop with plugins and extensions, additional payment methods, and WooCommerce themes. You may adjust every aspect of your web store to better reflect your company's values, your products, and your clients' tastes. Let's have a look at some methods and approaches that can help you take your online store to the next level in terms of functionality and customer experience.

Extending WooCommerce with plugins and extensions

Here, we'll take a look at some of the many plugins and extensions you may use to customize your WooCommerce store's features. You can tailor your online shop's appearance, functionality, and functionality with the help of these robust extensions. You may provide your consumers a one-of-a-kind and personalized shopping experience by carefully selecting and implementing the proper plugins and extensions. For a more in-depth look at how plugins and extensions might enrich your WooCommerce store, read on.

Understanding the Power of Plugins and Extensions

Plugins and extensions are add-on programs that work with WooCommerce without disrupting its normal operation. They are tailored to meet certain requirements and go above and beyond what is offered by WooCommerce itself. These extensions cater to a wide variety of needs, from marketing to customer service to logistics to data analysis to stock management and beyond. WooCommerce's adaptability and scalability mean that you may tailor your online store to meet the needs of your company with the help of these plugins and extensions.

Selecting the Right Plugins and Extensions

Choose plugins and extensions for your online store based on the features and capabilities you wish to implement. First, you should evaluate your company's requirements and pinpoint places where you might cut costs, delight customers, or expand your reach. Investigate and compare the many plugins and extensions provided by WooCommerce and other trustworthy third-party developers. Verify the plugins' dependability and compatibility with your WooCommerce installation by reading reviews, ratings, and support documentation from previous users.

Popular Plugin Categories and Examples

Let's have a look at some common types of plugins and some working examples:

Marketing and Promotions

These add-ons facilitate the launch of advertising initiatives, including newsletters, discounts, membership programs, and individualized suggestions. Integrations with social media and discount code generators are just a few examples.

Shipping and Fulfillment

These add-ons extend the functionality of your shipping process with features like real-time shipping pricing, label printing, and integrated tracking. Some examples are ShipStation, EasyPost, and WooCommerce Shipping.

Customer Experience

Plugins that add features like live chat, user reviews and ratings, specialized search and filtering, and wish lists can greatly improve a customer's time spent buying. WooCommerce has a product filter, and LiveChat and Yotpo are two other examples.

Analytics and Reporting

Your store's success may be monitored and analyzed with the help of various plugins that provide data on things like sales, customer behavior, and conversion rates. Metorik, Google Ads for WooCommerce, and the Google Analytics plugin are just a few examples.

Installing and Configuring Plugins and Extensions

Here are some guidelines for installing and setting up WooCommerce add-ons and plugins:

- Get the needed plugin or extension from a reliable vendor or download site.
- To install a new plugin, go to your WordPress admin area and choose "Plugins" > "Add New."
- Select the plugin file you downloaded and click the "Upload Plugin" button.
- To begin the installation, select "Install Now" and be patient while it finishes.

- After the add-on or plugin has been installed, it must be activated.
- Adjust the plugin's settings in accordance with your needs and preferences using the included documentation or setup wizard.

Regular Maintenance and Updates

Check for plugin and extension updates on a regular basis to ensure they are up to current. In order to enhance functionality, eliminate bugs, and guarantee compatibility with the most recent releases of WooCommerce and WordPress, developers frequently issue updates. If you want to take advantage of the latest and greatest features and security fixes, you should check the release notes and update your plugins on a regular basis.

By adding the appropriate plugins and extensions to WooCommerce, you can make a webshop that is tailored to your specific needs and those of your customers. Select and implement plugins and extensions with care, making sure they are compatible and reliable for your needs. Keep your plugins up-to-date and running smoothly to provide your consumers the best purchasing experience possible.

Implementing additional payment gateways

While WooCommerce does include some payment gateways, adding more allows you to accommodate a greater variety of customers and payment methods. Providing a variety of payment options improves the shopping cart experience, inspires client confidence, and drives sales growth. Let's get into the details of adding new payment options:

Assessing Payment Gateway Options

It's crucial to consider your intended market and your company's needs when deciding which additional payment gateways to use. Discover which major payment gateways are compatible with WooCommerce and take into account their transaction costs, supported countries and currencies, security measures, and integration options. Payment processors including PayPal, Stripe, Authorize.Net, Square, and Braintree are all widely used. Compare their available options and features to get the one that best suits your online store's needs.

Configuring the Chosen Payment Gateway

Once you've decided on a payment processor, set it up in your WooCommerce store by doing the following:

Create an Account

Join the preferred online payment system by creating an account with them. Please provide the requested details and carry out any necessary verification procedures.

Install the Payment Gateway Plugin

You may find the plugin for your preferred payment processor by going to "Plugins" > "Add New" in your WordPress dashboard. Get the add-on going by activating it.

Configure the Payment Gateway

Enter your credentials and the payment gateway's configuration information on the plugin's settings page. Some examples of such settings are API keys, secret keys, and information about a merchant account.

Test the Integration

You should run some test transactions to make sure everything is set up properly before making the payment gateway available to your clients. Verify that orders are being fulfilled, payments are being handled, and statuses are being updated.

Communicating Supported Payment Methods

Once you've added more payment channels, it's important to make sure your clients know exactly which ones you accept. Make sure the payment options and checkout page copy reflect the new gateways. Please specify which types of credit cards, electronic wallets, and other payment options are accepted. Customers may rest certain that their preferred payment option is safe and convenient thanks to this openness.

Security Considerations

Implementing payment gateways in your online store requires careful attention to security. Make sure the payment processors you use have high security standards and offer strong encryption. If you want to take advantage of the newest security fixes, you should update your WooCommerce and payment gateway plugins on a regular basis. Customers will feel more comfortable doing financial transactions with you if they see trust symbols like SSL certificates and security badges.

Customer Support and Dispute Resolution

It's crucial to be ready to support clients with any payment-related issues or enquiries while introducing new payment gateways. Learn the dispute resolution policies and contact information for the payment gateway. Maintain open lines of communication with your customers and act quickly to resolve any problems that may develop with their payments. Customers are more likely to return to your online store and do business with you if you provide them with clear communication and proactive support.

Additional payment gateways allow you to meet the needs of a wider range of customers, improve the shopping cart experience, and ultimately boost conversion rates. Pick a payment processor that works for your business and your customers. Make sure your clients are aware of the payment options available to them and that the selected payment gateway has been properly configured and tested. Protecting your customers' financial data should be a top priority, so be ready to answer any questions they may have about making a payment. Customers' confidence in your WooCommerce store will grow as a result of its streamlined and protected checkout experience.

Utilizing WooCommerce themes for advanced features

You may improve your online shop's aesthetics, user experience, and overall functionality with the help of a WooCommerce theme. Using the appropriate WooCommerce theme, you can build a beautiful and functional online store that attracts and retains customers. Let's go into the specifics of maximizing advanced features with WooCommerce themes:

Selecting the Right WooCommerce Theme

If you want your online store to look and function a certain way, picking the proper WooCommerce theme is essential.

When choosing a topic, keep in mind the following guidelines:

Responsive Design

Make sure the theme works properly on a wide range of devices by checking its responsiveness. Your clients will have a seamless and enjoyable surfing experience across all devices thanks to this.

WooCommerce Compatibility

Make sure the theme has been tested with WooCommerce and is compatible with it. This guarantees that all of WooCommerce's functions, like product listings, cart features, and checkout procedures, will work as intended.

Customization Options

Look into the theme's settings to make sure it will allow you to give your online store the exact look and feel you want. Try to find themes that let you play around with different hues, typefaces, and layouts.

Performance Optimization

Choose themes that have been optimized for performance for quick page loads and a fluid user experience. User happiness and search engine rankings both rise when using a theme that has been optimized to perfection.

Support and Updates

Verify if the theme creator provides ongoing support and updates. This guarantees that the theme will continue to work with future versions of WooCommerce and WordPress and that any defects will be fixed as soon as possible.

Key Advanced Features Provided by WooCommerce Themes

WooCommerce themes come with a plethora of useful extras that can make your online store more effective. Let's take a look at some of the more standard premium options offered by WooCommerce templates:

Product Showcase Layouts

Themes typically have grid or carousel layouts, editable product pages, and comparison tables to help you best present your wares to potential customers. These designs boost product exposure and provide a more pleasant shopping environment for your customers.

Advanced Filtering and Sorting

Customers can narrow their search by a variety of criteria, including price, size, color, and category with the help of sophisticated filtering and sorting capabilities provided by some themes. Customers are able to save time and effort thanks to the enhancements made to the product discovery process.

Mega Menus

With mega menus, you can make huge drop-down menus with multiple columns, perfect for displaying a broad variety of product types, subtypes, and promotional content. Mega menus make it easier to get around and make browsing more interesting to look at.

Integration with Page Builders

The popular Elementor and Beaver Builder page-building plugins are compatible with many WooCommerce themes. You don't need to know how to code in order to make landing pages, product showcases, or other unique layouts using this integration.

Enhanced Checkout Processes

One-step checkout processes and additional fields for collecting relevant consumer data are features offered by some themes. The shopping cart abandonment rate is lowered and conversion rates are raised thanks to these features.

Implementing and Customizing the Chosen Theme

Here's how to put into action and modify a WooCommerce theme you've chosen that fits your needs:

Install the Theme

Click "Appearance" > "Themes" in your WordPress dashboard to install the theme developer's file. The theme should be activated after installation.

Customize the Theme

You can modify the theme's appearance using the WordPress Customizer or its accompanying settings page. Alter the appearance of the site by changing the colors, the fonts, the header, and the footer.

Configure Theme-specific Features
It may be necessary to alter the settings or activate the options for some themes. If the theme comes with any advanced features, they should be set up in the same way as the documentation or support resources suggest.

Add Content and Products
Fill your online store with content and items using the theme's sophisticated tools and layouts. To improve the user experience as a whole, make sure your product listings, categorization structures, and written content all adhere to industry standards.

Regular Maintenance and Updates
Keep your selected theme up-to-date so you can take advantage of fixes, security updates, and new features as they become available. Keep a watch out for theme updates, and if one is released, install it according to the developer's documentation. When you keep up with routine maintenance, you can rest assured that your online store will always be safe, fast, and user-friendly.

With the help of WooCommerce themes, you can improve your online store's usability and aesthetics, giving your consumers a more satisfying shopping experience. Make sure the theme you choose is responsive and compatible with WooCommerce before launching your online store. Use the theme's powerful tools to create an engaging product presentation, simplify site navigation, and enhance the purchasing experience. Update and maintain your theme on a regular basis to take advantage of enhancements and guarantee a consistent user experience. Your online store's visibility and sales potential are directly tied to the quality of the WooCommerce theme you use.

6.   *Optimizing Your Webshop for Performance and Security*

Keeping your online store optimized for speed and safety is essential in today's interconnected world. Customer satisfaction, trust, and sales can all take a hit if your web store takes too long to load, has security holes, or is incompatible with popular browsers. The significance of webshop performance and security optimization will be discussed in this chapter. Methods including caching and speed optimization, safeguarding sensitive client information, and cross-browser and device compatibility will all be covered.

Keeping your online store's performance and security at peak levels is an ongoing effort that calls for constant monitoring, testing, and optimization. Create a quick, safe, and user-friendly web store by applying cache and speed optimization strategies, protecting your webshop from potential attacks, and checking for browser and device compatibility. Let's take a look at some ideas and recommendations for improving your online store's speed, security, and customer service.

Caching and optimizing your webshop's speed

One of the key factors that determine the success of your webshop is its speed and responsiveness. In today's fast-paced digital world, customers expect instant access to information and seamless browsing experiences. Slow loading times can lead to frustration, higher bounce rates, and a loss of potential customers. Here, we will explore the importance of caching and optimizing your webshop's speed. We will delve into various techniques and best practices that can significantly enhance the performance of your webshop. Let's dive into the details:

Understanding Caching

Caching plays a crucial role in speeding up your webshop by storing static content, such as images, CSS files, and JavaScript, in a temporary storage location. By caching these elements, subsequent page requests can be served from the cache instead of generating them dynamically each time. This significantly reduces the load on your server and improves page load times. We will explore different caching methods and how to implement them effectively.

Leveraging Browser Caching

Browser caching allows you to specify how long a web browser should cache certain files from your webshop. By setting appropriate cache expiration headers, you can instruct the browser to store static files locally, enabling faster subsequent page loads for returning visitors. We will discuss how to configure caching headers and leverage browser caching to enhance the speed and efficiency of your webshop.

Implementing Content Delivery Networks (CDNs)

Content Delivery Networks (CDNs) are distributed networks of servers located across different geographical regions. They store cached versions of your webshop's static content in multiple locations, ensuring faster delivery to users regardless of their location. We will explore the benefits of using CDNs and guide you through the process of integrating a CDN into your webshop to improve performance.

Minifying and Combining Files

Minification involves removing unnecessary characters, whitespace, and comments from your CSS, JavaScript, and HTML files. By minifying these files, you can significantly reduce their size and improve loading times. Additionally, combining multiple CSS and JavaScript files into a single file minimizes the number of requests required to load a page, further enhancing speed. We will discuss tools and techniques to minify and combine files effectively.

Optimizing Image Sizes and Formats

Images often contribute to the bulk of a webshop's page size and can slow down loading times. Optimizing image sizes by compressing and resizing them without sacrificing quality can have a substantial impact on speed. Additionally, choosing the appropriate image format, such as JPEG, PNG, or WebP, based on the specific content and level of compression required, further enhances performance. We will explore image optimization techniques and tools to help you strike the right balance between image quality and file size.

Regular Performance Monitoring and Testing

Optimizing your webshop's speed is an ongoing process. Regularly monitoring and testing its performance using tools like Google PageSpeed Insights or GTmetrix allows you to identify areas that need improvement and track the effectiveness of optimization efforts. We will guide you on how to interpret performance metrics, diagnose bottlenecks, and implement necessary optimizations based on the test results.

By implementing caching and optimizing your webshop's speed, you can provide a fast and seamless browsing experience for your customers. Improved speed leads to increased user satisfaction, lower bounce rates, and higher conversion rates. With a focus on caching techniques, leveraging browser caching, implementing CDNs, minifying and combining files, optimizing images, and regularly monitoring performance, you can create a high-performing webshop that keeps customers engaged and maximizes your business potential. Let's explore the strategies and best practices to boost your webshop's speed and deliver an exceptional user experience.

Implementing security measures and protecting customer data

Keeping your online store safe is essential if you want to earn your clients' trust and prevent any unwanted access to their personal information. The increasing sophistication of cyber attacks makes it all the more crucial that you take strong security precautions to safeguard your customers' data and keep your online store running smoothly. Here, we'll discuss why it's crucial to take precautions and follow industry standards when dealing with sensitive customer information. Let's get into the details:

Using Secure Communication Protocols (HTTPS)

Secure your online storefront by switching to HTTPS (Hypertext Transfer Protocol Secure). By using HTTPS, sensitive information such as login passwords, payment information, and personal details sent between a user's browser and your webserver are protected from eavesdropping. We'll go over how to get an SSL/TLS certificate and set up your server such that only HTTPS traffic is allowed.

Employing Strong Authentication Mechanisms

Protecting user accounts and thwarting hacking requires robust authentication mechanisms. Multi-factor authentication (MFA) should be implemented and complicated passwords should be encouraged. To log in with MFA enabled, users need to enter a password and a one-time verification code sent to their mobile device, for example. Several methods of authentication and their optimal implementation will be discussed.

Regularly Updating and Patching Software

Software updates are essential to the safety of your online store. Always use the most recent versions of your CMS, plugins, themes, and any other components to avoid security holes and bugs. Cybercriminals can exploit security holes in software that hasn't been updated in a while. We'll talk about why it's crucial to manage software updates efficiently and why updating on time is so important.

Encrypting Customer Data

The transfer and storage of sensitive customer information must be encrypted. You should encrypt your database to protect private information like credit card numbers and user profiles. We'll go through several kinds of encryption, such symmetric and asymmetric, and help you figure out how to put them to use to keep your customers' information safe.

Implementing Web Application Firewalls (WAFs)

Additional security is offered by online Application Firewalls (WAFs), which monitor and filter incoming online traffic. SQL injections, cross-site scripting (XSS) assaults, and brute-force login attempts are just some of the dangerous activities they can detect and prevent. We'll go over why WAFs are useful, and then show you how to set one up for your online store.

Conducting Regular Security Audits and Vulnerability Assessments

The security of your online store can be improved by routinely testing it for vulnerabilities and conducting security audits. Assessments like this conduct vulnerability scans and penetration tests on your online store to mimic actual attacks. We'll delve into why these evaluations are so crucial, and offer pointers for how to carry them out correctly.

Educating and Training Your Staff

The most common cause of security failures is human mistake. Staff members must be educated and trained on security best practices to ensure they know their roles and duties in keeping your online store safe. In this context, "password hygiene," "phishing awareness," and "safe browsing habits" are all possible topics to discuss. We will talk about the value of training your employees and offer suggestions for fostering a security-conscious company culture.

Trust from clients can be earned and kept by taking strong security precautions to preserve their personal information. Secure communication protocols, strong authentication mechanisms, frequent software updates and patches, encryption of client data, implementation of web application firewalls, regular security audits and vulnerability assessments, and employee education should all be priorities. You may provide your consumers peace of mind and protect your online store by following these steps. Let's take a look at how you can better secure your online store and keep your customers' information safe.

Ensuring compatibility with different browsers and devices

With so many different browsers and devices in use, it's more important than ever to test for compatibility to guarantee a good shopping experience for all of your customers. Your webstore needs to be accessible and functional across a wide range of browsers and devices. Learn why it's crucial to test your site on a variety of browsers and devices in this section. We will talk about methods and recommendations for improving webshop compatibility and usability. Let's get into the details:

Embrace Responsive Web Design

To guarantee compatibility across all devices, responsive web design is a must. Incorporating responsive web design into your online store's development ensures a top-notch browsing experience across desktops, tablets, and mobile phones. Here, we'll delve into responsive web design's foundational ideas and offer practical advice for putting them into practice.

Perform Cross-Browser Testing

Cross-browser testing is vital to guarantee compatibility across browsers. Make sure your webstore works and looks the same in Chrome, Firefox, Safari, and Edge as it does on any other browser. We'll go over methods and resources for browser compatibility testing, and help you figure out how to fix any problems that crop up.

Optimize for Mobile Devices

With more and more people using their mobile devices to access the internet and make purchases online, mobile optimization of your webshop is essential. The term "mobile optimization" refers to the process of tailoring your online store's structure, navigation, and content to the needs of customers using mobile devices. To guarantee a pleasurable experience for mobile users, we will investigate mobile optimization tactics like touch-friendly interfaces, streamlined navigation, and quicker load times.

Follow Accessibility Guidelines

Increasing your online store's accessibility means making it more user-friendly for people with different abilities. By adhering to accessibility standards, you increase the likelihood that customers with disabilities, such as those affecting sight or mobility, will be able to use and enjoy your online store. Alternative language for images, appropriate header layouts, and keyboard accessibility are just a few of the topics we'll cover as we dive into accessibility best practices.

Optimize Page Load Speed

A favorable user experience must be maintained across a wide range of devices and browsers, making fast page load times crucial. Minimize web store load times by optimizing code and pictures and making use of caching strategies. Here, we'll go into methods to speed up page loads and offer advice on how to fine-tune your online store.

Test on Different Devices

In addition to cross-browser testing, making sure your web store works properly on a range of devices is essential. This guarantees a unified design and seamless functionality across all platforms. To help you verify device compatibility, we'll go over some testing methodologies and tools.

Stay Updated with Technology Advancements

New browsers, gadgets, and technologies appear frequently and contribute to the ever-changing nature of the digital realm. Maintain compatibility with current web standards by keeping up with developments in the field. Keep abreast of developing technologies like progressive web applications (PWAs) and responsive images that can further boost compatibility by testing your web store on new browser versions on a regular basis.

You can attract more customers and improve the quality of your webshop's user experience by testing it on a variety of browsers and devices. Use techniques like responsive web design, cross-browser testing, mobile optimization, adherence to accessibility rules, page speed optimization, device testing, and knowledge of the latest technological developments to ensure success. If you follow these guidelines, you'll be able to build a web store that works well for customers on any browser or device. We'll go over some tips and tricks for making your online store fully compatible and user-friendly.

7. *Marketing and Promoting Your Webshop*

In this chapter, we'll dive into how to improve your webshop's speed and security, two factors that are crucial to providing a satisfying shopping experience for your customers and growing your business. Customers will have a more pleasurable and worry-free purchasing experience if you take the time to optimize your webshop for speed, apply strong security measures, and test for browser and device compatibility.

Improving client satisfaction, credibility, and sales may all be accomplished through performance and security optimization of your online store. Your web store's responsiveness, page load speeds, and user engagement will all improve with the implementation of caching and speed optimization measures. Customers will have more faith in your company and its products if they know their information is secure from prying eyes. Your web store's accessibility and user experience will benefit from being optimized for several browsers and devices. In order to provide your customers with a safe and secure online buying experience, it is important to optimize your webshop for performance and security.

Implementing SEO strategies for better visibility

Search engine optimization (SEO) is essential for bringing in new visitors from the web and making sales. Structure, content, and technical factors can all be optimized to boost your online store's visibility in search results and attract customers looking for what you're selling. Let's get into the weeds of optimizing your site for search engines:

Understanding the Basics of SEO

Search engine optimization (SEO) is a set of procedures and guidelines designed to raise a website's position in SERPs. On-page and off-page optimization techniques are included. Off-page optimization includes constructing high-quality backlinks and developing your website's authority in the sector, while on-page optimization focuses on optimizing your webshop's content, meta tags, headings, and URL structure. Both contribute to raising the profile and popularity of your online store in SERPs.

Keyword Research and Optimization

SEO novices should not skip keyword research. The process is figuring out what people are actually typing into search engines to find goods and services like yours. Incorporating high-traffic, relevant keywords into your online store's content, product descriptions, meta tags, and headlines is a certain way to boost your site's visibility and attract more customers. This optimization increases your webstore's discoverability by assisting search engines in determining its relevance to individual inquiries.

Optimizing Webshop Structure and Navigation

Customers and search engines alike will appreciate a web store that is easy to navigate. Be sure that your online store's categories, subcategories, and internal links all make sense and lead customers to the content they're looking for quickly and easily. Breadcrumb navigation can assist users and search engines better comprehend your site's hierarchy. Make your URLs user-friendly and easy to read by optimizing their structure to contain relevant keywords.

Compelling and Unique Product Descriptions

You should strive for originality and clarity while writing product descriptions. If you want to improve your search engine rankings, you should avoid utilizing manufacturer-provided descriptions that are identical on various websites. Create compelling and unique product descriptions that do justice to your items by describing them in detail, highlighting their best characteristics, and organically incorporating relevant keywords. Product descriptions that are both informative and engaging are more likely to result in a purchase.

Optimizing Images and Multimedia

Adding images and other forms of media can do wonders for your online store's aesthetics. However, if they aren't optimized appropriately, they can slow down page loads. Reduce the size of your photographs without losing quality by compressing them, and give them meaningful names and alt tags. This enhancement makes images more accessible for users with visual impairments and helps search engines better interpret their information. Lazy loading approaches, in which images are loaded only when they are visible to the user, can be used to increase page load speed.

Mobile Optimization

In today's mobile-first society, optimizing for mobile devices is critical. Due to the rise in mobile device usage, search engines now provide higher results to mobile-friendly websites. Make sure that customers can easily shop on any device, regardless of screen size, by making your online store responsive. Reduce code size, compress pictures, and use caching to improve mobile page load times. Make sure your online store is optimized for mobile use by conducting usability tests on various platforms.

Monitoring and Analytics

Use an analytics program, such as Google Analytics, to keep tabs on how well your online store is doing. Examine metrics like keyword ranks, bounce rates, and sales conversion rates in addition to organic search traffic volumes. You may use the results of this investigation to pinpoint problem areas, monitor the efficacy of your search engine optimization tactics, and make educated judgments about how best to enhance the performance of your online store.

By optimizing your online store for search engines, you may boost its exposure, pull in more organic traffic, and improve your chances of making a sale. Search engine optimization (SEO) is a never-ending process that can be driven by thorough keyword research and optimization, optimized webshop structure and navigation, unique product descriptions, optimized images and multimedia, a focus on mobile optimization, and regular monitoring of your webshop's performance.

Utilizing social media integration to drive traffic

You can market your business, connect with potential consumers, and reach a large audience all at once by using a social networking platform. You may boost your web shop's visibility, name recognition, and traffic by incorporating social media into it. Let's get into the details of how to increase traffic using social media integration:

Choosing the Right Social Media Platforms

Determine which social media sites are the best fit for reaching your ideal customers and achieving your company's goals. Think about social media sites and websites like these: Facebook, Instagram, Twitter, Pinterest, LinkedIn, and YouTube. It is crucial to choose the platforms that most appeal to your target audience in terms of their features and demographics. Put in the most time and effort into the channels where your intended audience spends the most time and energy.

Integrating Social Media Buttons and Sharing Features

Add sharing buttons to your online store to get people talking about your business online. Put these links in obvious places like the header and footer, or right on the product pages themselves. You may expand the reach of your web store by encouraging customers to share your products and content with their social media followers using built-in social sharing options. Add sharing buttons to your website, blog entries, and other information that can be easily shared with others.

Showcasing Social Proof and User-Generated Content

Use user-generated material and social proof to win people over and get them involved. Integrate social network feeds or client testimonials into your online store to highlight the good experiences and interactions your business has fostered. Get your consumers talking about your business on social media by showcasing user-generated material like product reviews and comments. This not only establishes credibility, but also fosters solidarity and veracity.

Creating Engaging Social Media Content

Create material for your social media accounts that reflects your brand's values and will appeal to your intended audience. Make material that people will want to talk about, like videos, how-to tutorials, customer testimonials, exclusive content, and news about your products and services. Use attention-grabbing images, clever captions, and trending hashtags to get people talking. Publish useful and engaging material on a regular basis to attract customers to your online store.

Running Social Media Campaigns and Contests

Create a stir, boost participation, and send people to your online store by running a campaign or a contest on social media. You could, for instance, hold a contest in which entrants' social media shares would count toward entry. Get people to enter by sharing the contest on social media, following your accounts, and shopping at your online store. This tactic does double duty by increasing exposure and the number of people following your social media accounts.

Collaborating with Influencers and Partners

Working with influential people and similar companies can do wonders for your online store's exposure and foot traffic. Locate prominent opinion leaders in your field who are actively communicating with your intended audience. Work together to advertise both of your companies' wares. By working together, you can reach more people, build trust in your brand, and get more people to visit your online store.

Analyzing and Optimizing Social Media Performance

Use platform analytics and tools like Google Analytics to monitor the efficacy of your social media marketing on a regular basis. Keep an eye on key performance indicators including audience size, time spent on site, clickthroughs, and sales. Determine which social media channels and content formats are most successful in bringing customers to your online store. Make better decisions about your social media strategies, content, and platform investments with this information.

By properly incorporating social media into your online store, you can take advantage of the platforms' huge potential to boost traffic, raise brand awareness, and attract new customers. You can increase your webshop's traffic and sales by utilizing the power of social media in such ways as strategic button placement, social sharing features, showcasing social proof, creating engaging content, running campaigns and contests, collaborating with influencers, and analyzing performance.

Running promotions, discounts, and loyalty programs

These promotional efforts succeed in drawing in new buyers, encouraging existing ones to buy more often, and strengthening relationships with existing clients. Customers can be enticed to visit your online store, make more purchases, and become loyal patrons if you provide them with enticing discounts, prizes, and other incentives. Let's go into the details of discounting, couponing, and membership programs:

Benefits of Promotions, Discounts, and Loyalty Programs

The benefits of running sales, discounts, and customer loyalty programs for your online store are numerous. They instill a sense of urgency and enthusiasm in buyers, encouraging them to make a quick decision. Additionally, these actions set your company apart from rivals and inspire consumer loyalty. Loyalty programs have shown to boost client retention, encourage repeat purchases, and spread good word of mouth. Discounts and other sales can help bring in new consumers and spread the word about your online store.

Types of Promotions and Discounts

In your online store, you can run a number of different sales and discount events. Here are some frequent ones:

Percentage or Dollar-Off Discounts

Give a price cut as a percentage, a flat rate, or an absolute dollar amount on some or all of the items in the shopping cart.

Free Shipping

Offer free shipping on all orders, or for a limited time if the customer spends above a particular amount.

Buy One, Get One (BOGO)

Give something away or reduce the price of something else when you buy it.

Flash Sales

Hold flash sales at huge discounts for a short period of time.

Seasonal Promotions

Market your products or services by associating them with special occasions.

Limited-Time Offers

Discounts and limited-time deals can generate this sense of urgency.

Loyalty Programs and Rewards

Having a customer loyalty program in place can encourage customers to come back and spend more. Methods used in loyalty programs include:

Points-Based Programs

Give your customers points for making purchases and let them use those points to buy anything at a discount or even for free stuff.

Tiered Programs

Create several tiers based on a customer's spending or participation, with higher tiers receiving more perks and access to unique prizes.

Referral Programs

Incentives like discounts or store credits can be offered to customers who refer their friends and family to your online store.

Birthday Rewards

Give your consumers a reason to celebrate by giving them a discount or a unique promotion on their birthday.

Promotion and Loyalty Program Management

It's crucial to properly manage and disseminate information about loyalty and promotional programs. Take into account the following options:

Clear Promotion Guidelines

Promoted items and services should have their limitations, expiration dates, and redemption procedures made clear.

Promotion Timing

Plan your marketing campaigns strategically so that they coincide with peak shopping times, holidays, or other occasions that will appeal to your customer base.

Personalization

To better serve your customers, you should personalize your promos and rewards depending on their likes, purchases, and involvement in loyalty programs.

Marketing and Communication

Use tools like email marketing, social media, and website banners to spread the word about your discounts and loyalty programs. Make it very clear to customers what benefits they will reap from taking part.

Tracking and Analysis

Use analytics tools to track the success of your marketing campaigns and customer retention initiatives. In order to evaluate their efficacy and make informed adjustments, keep tabs on KPIs like consumer engagement, repeat purchases, and redemption rates.

Maintaining Fairness and Transparency

Maintain your customers' faith by running honest and open loyalty and discount programs. Spell out the details, including who is eligible and how to redeem your prize. Don't do anything to make customers doubt your web store's integrity.

You may expand your customer base, encourage current customers to spend more, and strengthen your bonds with them all through the use of loyalty programs, discounts, and special offers. Exciting customers, increasing sales, and cementing relationships with loyal customers may all be accomplished with the help of promotions and loyalty programs. Your initiatives will have the greatest possible effect if they are managed, communicated, and analyzed in an efficient manner.

8. Monitoring and Analyzing Your Webshop's Performance

In this chapter, we'll discuss why it's crucial to keep an eye on your online store's stats with the use of analytics software. You may improve the efficiency of your webstore by taking advantage of the data you collect about your site's visitors, purchases, and other vital metrics. By keeping tabs on and analyzing data, you may learn more about your customers' likes and dislikes, pinpoint problem areas, and take preventative steps to boost your online store's efficiency.

Keeping an eye on your online store's stats will help you remain ahead of the competition, spot areas for expansion, and boost customer happiness. Decisions about your webstore's direction might be driven by data analytics, data interpretation, and optimization tactics. Discover the key to unlocking your webstore's full potential through regular performance monitoring and analysis.

Using analytics tools to track visitor behavior and sales

It's vital to your online store's success that you analyze visitor behavior and sales statistics. Data-driven decisions can be made to optimize your webstore's performance once you acquire useful insights into how visitors interact with your site through the use of analytics tools and the monitoring of key indicators. In this section, we'll discuss the value of employing analytics software to monitor site traffic and revenue. Let's get into the details:

Choosing the Right Analytics Tools

Selecting the proper analytics platform for your webstore is the first step in monitoring customer activity and sales. Google Analytics is widely used because of its convenient interface and extensive set of capabilities. Traffic, user activity, conversion rates, and revenue are just few of the metrics that may be gleaned from the data. Additional functionality can be found in other analytics platforms like Kissmetrics, Mixpanel, and Adobe Analytics. Select an analytics platform that helps you measure what matters most to your company, such as customer engagement and conversion rates.

Implementing Analytics Tracking Codes

Once an analytics tool has been selected, the tracking code must be added to the online store. The analytics tool supplies the tracking code, which is a small amount of JavaScript. Because of this, the gadget may track users' actions and relay that information for further review. Make sure the tracking code loads on all pages by putting it in the header or footer of your online store. Verify the correct operation of the tracking by testing the implemented solution.

Tracking Key Metrics

You can monitor things like visitor activity and sales with the help of analytics tools. Here are a few of the most important metrics:

Website Traffic

Keep an eye on how many people are visiting your online store, where they're coming from (organic, direct, referral, etc.), and what they're searching for.

User Engagement

You can learn a lot about how people use your webstore and how they respond to your content by monitoring metrics like average time on site, bounce rate, and page views per session.

Conversion Rates

Keep an eye on your conversion rates for things like form submissions, purchases, and newsletter subscriptions. You'll be able to fix any conversion problems with your online store that this reveals.

Sales and Revenue

Keep an eye on metrics like total sales, AOV, and CR to see how well your business is doing. Examine the results of marketing initiatives by analyzing sales data and determining which goods are most successful.

Setting Up Goals and Funnels

With the help of goals and funnels, you can monitor and evaluate various user paths. Define objectives that are in line with your webstore's aims, such as a successful purchase, newsletter subscription, or contact form submission. The steps that customers take to complete an action can be mapped out with the aid of a funnel. Goals and conversion funnels help you track where visitors are dropping off so you can fix the problem areas and boost conversions.

Analyzing User Behavior

Data analytics programs let you see how customers interact with your online store. Examine data like pageviews, session duration, and clickthrough rates to find out which content is most popular and which needs work. Determine the most frequented starting and ending points in order to improve navigation and user satisfaction. You may further visualize how customers use your webstore by using tools like heatmaps and user recordings to learn where improvements can be made.

Monitoring E-commerce Data

It is essential to monitor key e-commerce indicators if you run an online store. In order to measure data like product views, add-to-cart percentages, and transaction values, you need to set up e-commerce tracking in your analytics solution. Use this information to zero in on hot sellers, deduce customer preferences, and fine-tune your price and supply chain.

You can learn a lot about how well your online store is doing from the data collected through analytics tools. Better user experiences, more conversions, and better business outcomes can all result from analyzing important indicators, putting up goals and funnels, and monitoring e-commerce data. Discovering growth prospects and optimizing your web store's performance are both facilitated by analytics.

Interpreting data and making informed decisions

Next, you'll need to analyse the data and draw useful conclusions after you've set up analytics tools and begun tracking key indicators for your webstore. Your web store's performance, your customers' experiences, and your bottom line can all be enhanced through data analysis. The value of data interpretation and sound decision making is discussed here. Let's get into the details:

Understand Your Business Objectives

Understanding your webstore's business goals is crucial before digging into data interpretation. Make a list of your desired outcomes and the KPIs that will help you get there. With this understanding, you can direct your data analysis toward the KPIs that really matter for your online store's health.

Identify Patterns and Trends

You can learn a lot about how your online store is doing by analyzing the data you collect. Examine metrics like peak traffic times, product categories, and high-converting landing pages to identify trends in user engagement. Examine the trajectory of measurements to see if they are increasing or decreasing over time. You may learn a lot about what your users like and don't like by observing these trends and patterns.

Segment Data for Deeper Insights

By dividing your audience into smaller subsets, you may learn more about each subset and how they interact with your site. You can segment your information by user age, gender, location, device used, and referral source. You can learn more about user behavior, your audience, and how to best serve them by comparing the success of various segments.

Identify Conversion Bottlenecks

Conversion bottlenecks, or instances in the customer journey where visitors drop off or fail to complete required actions, are one of the key targets of data interpretation. Examine your online store's sales channels and customer paths to identify these points of friction. It could be due to a number of factors, including an inefficient checkout procedure, unclear directions, or insufficient product details. Once you know where to look for optimization opportunities, you can take specific steps to boost conversions.

A/B Testing and Experimentation

The ability to evaluate data is also useful for performing studies and split-tests. You can learn which elements are most well-received by your target audience by comparing the results of numerous variations, such as page layouts, CTA buttons, and pricing methods. With the help of A/B testing, you can optimize your online store and your customers' online shopping experiences based on hard facts.

Use Data to Drive Personalization

Use collected information to tailor your online store to each individual customer. Make better product suggestions, customized content, and targeted ads with the help of data analysis. Engagement, client loyalty, and conversions can all be boosted by personalizing each visitor's experience based on their preferences and past activities.

Keep Up with Industry Trends

Data analysis should be performed often to track industry shifts and customer preferences. Keep an eye on things like visitor engagement levels and conversion rates as they change. Keep up with the latest market and customer trends, as well as emerging technologies. You may use this information to make strategic adjustments, capture fresh opportunities, and stay one step ahead of the competition.

Your web store's performance, your customers' experiences, and your bottom line can all benefit from your careful analysis of available data and the decisions you make as a result. Using data analysis, you may find trends, pinpoint obstacles to conversion, test hypotheses, and tailor your interactions with the company. Proactively examine data on a regular basis so that you may adjust your plans to meet the needs of your customers. The success of your online store can be catalyzed by the decisions you make with the help of data interpretation.

Optimizing your webshop based on insights gained

Your online store's success, visitor habits, and sales patterns can all be better understood with the use of data analysis. After analyzing the data and drawing conclusions, you can go on to improving your online store. You may improve the user experience, boost conversions, and maximize the efficiency of your web store by being proactive and making changes based on data. Here, we'll discuss why it's crucial to use your newfound knowledge to improve your online store. Let's get into the details:

Improve Website Design and Navigation

The study of data could uncover problem spots or points of misunderstanding for tourists. Take advantage of this knowledge to make your online storefront more user-friendly. Simplify the user experience, reduce the number of options available, and make the site easy to navigate. Place critical features like search fields, shopping carts, and contact information in the most convenient locations. An improved user experience and greater participation are the results of careful web design and intuitive navigation.

Enhance Product Descriptions and Imagery

Using data analysis, you can see which goods or categories are successful and which need want some tweaking. Apply this knowledge to enhance your product writing and photography. Make sure that the descriptions of your products are concise, detailed, and interesting to read. Make sure you're using high-quality product photos that do the actual goods justice. You may learn what kind of product descriptions and images your customers respond to best by conducting A/B tests.

Optimize Page Load Speed

Analysis of your data may show that your online store's page loads take too long, which can have a detrimental effect on consumer satisfaction and conversion rates. Reduce page load times in your online store by optimizing server response times, caching strategies, picture compression, and code simplification. Keep an eye on load times and conversion rates after making these changes to fine-tune the user experience.

Streamline the Checkout Process

Cart abandonment can be prevented by analyzing data from the checkout process to find places of friction. Simplify the checkout procedure by reducing the number of steps required, enabling guest checkout, and adjusting the placement of form fields. Provide a variety of payment methods to meet the needs of a wide range of customers. Conversion rates can be increased by regularly monitoring the checkout funnel for points of friction and fixing them.

Implement Personalization Strategies

Apply the knowledge you've obtained from data analysis to your online store's personalisation methods. Make use of visitor preferences, browsing behavior, and purchase history to tailor product recommendations, promotions, and content. By providing each visitor with content that is specifically designed for them, personalization improves the user experience, boosts engagement, and boosts conversions.

Continuously Test and Iterate

The process of optimizing is never finished. You may regularly test and improve different aspects of your webstore by using A/B testing and experimenting. The best layout, CTA, pricing, or product placement can only be determined by rigorous testing. Optimize your online store by keeping close tabs on key performance indicators and acting on the information you get.

Stay Responsive to Customer Feedback

Though data analysis is useful for its quantitative insights, it is also crucial to take into account the qualitative comments made by customers. Keeping an eye on customer feedback, questions, and social media comments can help you identify problems and address issues your clients are having. Make use of this information to guide your optimization efforts and concentrate on making changes that truly matter to your customers.

By continuously enhancing the user experience, increasing conversions, and driving business growth, you may use insights gathered through data analysis to optimize your webshop. Pay attention to website layout and usability, product descriptions and images, page load speed, the checkout process, personalisation methods, testing, and iteration. Maintain open communication with your customers and tailor your optimization strategies to their specific requirements and preferences. Using a data-driven optimization strategy, you can build a webstore that is both extremely efficient and focused on your customers' needs, making it stand out in the crowded e-commerce space.

9. *Troubleshooting and Maintenance*

In addition to developing and releasing a web store, maintenance, troubleshooting, and upkeep are all essential parts of keeping it running well. In this section, we will discuss the significance of webshop maintenance and troubleshooting. We'll go over potential problems and offer advice on how to fix them. We will also discuss the relevance of keeping your webstore up to date, as well as the importance of backing up and restoring your webshop's data.

You can ensure the continued health and viability of your webstore by familiarizing yourself with the most prevalent problems and their solutions, creating regular backups of your data, and installing any necessary updates. Maintaining a secure, fast, and error-free online store requires ongoing maintenance and troubleshooting. Let's take a look at the tools, procedures, and best practices for fixing bugs, backing up, and restoring your web store to ensure its survival and growth.

Common issues and how to resolve them

While opening up shop online has many potential benefits, it is not uncommon for problems to arise that can hinder business. To keep your web store running smoothly and successfully, you need to be aware of and able to efficiently address these typical concerns. Here, we'll discuss some of the most typical problems encountered by online store owners and offer specific recommendations for how to fix them. Let's get into the details:

Website Downtime

Many things can cause a website to go down, including problems with the server, incompatible software, or a malfunctioning network. In the event of a website outage, verifying the server and network connection is the first step. Make sure your hosting company is aware of the problem and taking steps to fix it. Take preventative measures by installing a monitoring system that sends out alerts in the event of downtime.

Slow Loading Times

When pages take too long to load, visitors become frustrated and leave the site. Start by compressing your photos, trimming your CSS and JavaScript files, and using caching techniques to speed up your site's loading times. One option for speedy content distribution is to use a CDN. In addition, use tools like Google PageSpeed Insights to assess your web store's performance, discover bottlenecks, and optimize as required.

Broken Links

Users' experiences and the store's usability can be negatively affected by broken links. Use broken link checkers or website auditing tools regularly to ensure there are no broken links on your site. As soon as you discover a broken link, you should either update the URL or redirect it to the appropriate page. If you want your visitors to have a pleasant browsing experience, you should check the links on your site regularly.

Payment Gateway Errors

In the event of a problem with the payment gateway, clients may become frustrated and abandon their carts. First, make sure the credentials you entered when connecting to the payment gateway are right. Validate your SSL certificate and make sure it is set up correctly to ensure safe financial transactions. For information on how to fix this error, contact your payment gateway service.

Plugin or Theme Compatibility Issues

When two plugins or themes interact poorly, your online store may suddenly stop working. If you're having compatibility problems, try updating your plugins and themes to the most recent versions. If the problem remains after these steps, you may need to temporarily revert to the site's default theme or disable plugins. If you need help with a plugin or theme, contact the creators of those tools or think about hiring web development experts.

Security Breaches

Customer information and your online store's reputation are both at risk if hackers gain access. Finding and stopping the origin of a security breach is the first step in fixing the problem. Users should immediately change their passwords and close any compromised accounts. Web application firewalls (WAFs), strong passwords, and regular software upgrades are all essential security steps to take. To evaluate and improve your webstore's security, you may want to consult with experts in the field of cybersecurity.

SEO Ranking Drops

The visibility and traffic of your online store can take a hit if it suddenly falls in the search engine results. Investigate the factors that may have contributed to the decline, such as updates to search engine algorithms, penalties, or technological problems. You may increase traffic to your online store by focusing on relevant keywords, removing broken links, increasing the quality of your content, and increasing the speed of your website. Always keep an eye on how well your SEO is performing and make adjustments as needed.

You can keep your web store running smoothly and successfully if you know how to identify and fix the most typical problems that customers encounter. Common problems can be fixed, such as website outages, slow loading times, broken links, payment gateway difficulties, plugin or theme compatibility issues, weakened security, and optimized search engine rankings. If you apply these methods, your online store will be more trustworthy and convenient for your clients.

Backing up and restoring your webshop

If you want to protect your online store against things like data loss, security breaches, and natural catastrophes, you need to back up your data regularly and have a solid restoration strategy in place. Maintaining frequent backups of your webstore's data is essential in the event of a data loss or other disaster. The significance of data backups and how to create and restore backups for your web store will be discussed here. Let's dive right into the details:

Importance of Regular Backups

The data on your web store should be backed up regularly. They're like insurance in case something goes wrong, like losing data or having technology malfunction or being hacked. Restoring your online store to its original state from a backup helps keep your data safe and secure while minimizing disruption to your business operations.

Choosing a Backup Method

You may safeguard your online store's information using a variety of backup strategies. There are several types of backups, such as complete, incremental, and remote. When you do an incremental backup, just the new or changed data since the last full backup is saved. An extra safeguard against data loss, corruption, or theft is provided by off-site backups, which are copies of your data stored in a remote place.

Selecting a Backup Schedule

If you want to reliably back up your data on a regular basis, you need to establish a backup routine. How often you back up your webstore relies on its data and how often it is updated. Depending on the amount and significance of your data, you may want to back it up once a day, once a week, or once a month. Finding a happy medium between keeping data safe and spending too much time and energy on backups is essential.

Backing Up Website Files and Databases

It is crucial to store both your website files and database backups separately. Databases maintain crucial information like customer details, order data, and product data, whereas website files include all the code, media, and other elements that make up your webshop. If you want to be able to restore everything in the event of a data loss, your backup strategy must include both.

Storing Backups Securely

Secure locations are recommended for storing backups to prevent theft, data loss, or destruction. Protect your backups from prying eyes by storing them in encrypted media either locally or in the cloud. Password-protect the backups so that only authorized users can access and restore them.

Testing Backup Restoration

If you want to make sure your backups are actually usable, you should restore from them on a regular basis. To make sure your backups are comprehensive and can be restored successfully, you should test them periodically in a separate environment. This method is useful for anticipatorily fixing any backup-related difficulties that may arise.

Documenting and Updating Backup Procedures

For the sake of uniformity and convenience, it is crucial to keep complete documentation of your backup methods. Make sure you have a written record of everything you need to back up and restore your online store. As your online store develops or as new technologies and best practices emerge, it is important to regularly assess and update your backup protocols.

To keep your online store's information secure and readily accessible at all times, develop a solid backup and restore strategy. You should create regular backups of your website's files and databases, store backups safely, test restoration procedures, and keep thorough documentation. Your online store's continued operation and your customers' faith in you depend on your ability to use these best practices to prevent data loss and bounce back quickly from setbacks.

Keeping your webshop up to date

In order to keep your online store running smoothly, securely, and in line with current industry norms and emerging technology, you must execute regular updates. Your online store's continued success, security from exploits, and access to enhanced functionality all depend on your keeping it up-to-date. We'll go through why it's crucial that your online store always be current, and how to handle updates, in the following sections. Let's get into the details:

Importance of Updates

Maintaining a safe and efficient online store relies heavily on keeping up with the latest updates. Updates typically consist of security patches, bug fixes, and performance enhancements that fix previously discovered flaws and make the program run smoother and more efficiently. Keeping your online store current protects your clients against known vulnerabilities, boosts performance, and guarantees a smooth transaction every time.

Update Your Content Management System (CMS)

The CMS, like WordPress, in the center of your online store is its most important component. Updating your content management system on a regular basis will give you access to the most recent bug fixes and functionality updates. Updating your content management system is essential for fixing security flaws and maintaining backwards compatibility with add-ons and skins.

Update Plugins and Themes

Your online store's functionality and aesthetic can be expanded with the help of plugins and themes. Maintaining the most recent version ensures you have access to the most recent features and fixes any security issues that may occur. Keep your plugins and themes up-to-date, checking for compatibility with your CMS version and reading the developers' release notes and documentation before making any changes.

Check for Plugin and Theme Compatibility

Make sure any updates to your plugins or themes are compatible with your CMS release before installing them. Some patches won't work with older software or may only function with certain configurations. Before pushing out changes to your live webstore, you should put them through their paces in a staging area to check for incompatibilities and identify potential points of contention.

Backup Your Webshop Before Updating

It is essential to create a backup of your web store's files and databases before making any changes. Having a backup means you can revert to a working state in the event of problems or conflicts during the updating process. Maintaining regular backups gives you extra security and peace of mind during software updates.

Follow Update Best Practices

It's important to use best practices while making changes to your online store in order to keep downtime to a minimum. To lessen the impact on users, updates should preferably be implemented at off-peak times. Security upgrades should be a top priority so that any flaws may be fixed as soon as possible. Before pushing changes to the production online store, try them out in a staging area.

Monitor and Test After Updates

It is essential to check on your online store's performance and functionality after making changes. Verify the functionality of the entire site by testing its most important functions and looking for bugs and inconsistencies. Keep an eye out for any bugs or performance issues that may have shown up on your online store after applying the changes.

Your online store's security, speed, and compatibility can all benefit from regular updates. You should always use the most recent versions of your content management system (CMS), plugins, and themes. Be sure to back up your online store frequently, always update in stages, and always follow best practices to ensure as little downtime as possible. Make sure everything is running well by testing your online store after any updates. Maintaining your online store's security and compatibility with current standards in the industry is as simple as being pro-active with updates. Let's take a look at some of the methods that have proven successful in managing web store updates.

10. Scaling and Growing Your Webshop

When your online store begins to develop popularity and clients, you'll need a plan for expanding to meet demand. To scale, you must grow your product offerings, streamline your inventory management practices, and test your online store's capacity to accommodate additional traffic and sales. This chapter delves into the fundamentals of expanding and scaling your online store. We'll talk about how to enhance your online store's inventory, streamline stock management, and boost capacity to meet rising customer demand.

You may set yourself up for growth and success by improving your product selection, inventory management, and e-commerce website so that it can handle more visitors and more sales. A larger consumer base may be attracted by offering more products, and operations can run smoothly thanks to careful inventory management. The ability to scale your web store's infrastructure in response to rising demand without decreasing service quality is a key selling point. Let's talk about how to make your web store bigger and better, so that it can compete more effectively in today's online economy.

Strategies for expanding your product range

Growing your webstore and appealing to a wider audience requires you to offer more products. Having a larger product range does wonders for your online store's potential for making sales and general attractiveness to customers. Here, we'll discuss several tried-and-true methods for broadening your product catalog in a way that still serves your existing clientele and attracts new ones. Let's start digging a little deeper into this topic:

Conduct Market Research

Conducting market research is essential for figuring out what consumers want, what consumers are buying, and what chances exist for new products. Determine what additional items would interest your target market by conducting research on their needs, preferences, and the current state of the market. You may learn more about your consumers' wants and needs by surveying them, interacting with them on social media, and keeping an eye on relevant industry forums.

Examine the Services Offered by Rivals

By examining what the competition is selling, you can learn what the market needs and where you can fill the void with your own goods. Look into their wares, pricing models, and client feedback. Find ways to set your online store apart by providing things that no one else does that will appeal to your niche market.

Source New Products

As soon as product openings have been found, investigate potential suppliers. To gain access to a broader selection of goods, you may want to form partnerships with new suppliers, manufacturers, or distributors. Going to trade shows and other industry events can help you meet suppliers and discover new products that are a good fit for your online store's image and customer base.

Create Partnerships

Partnerships with other companies allow you to provide more products and reach a wider audience. Establish mutually beneficial relationships with companies that sell goods and services compatible with those sold on your online store. Those in the clothing industry could benefit from teaming up with those in the accessory and shoe industries to offer bundles and promote each other's wares.

Introduce New Varieties of the Product

Variations of existing products are another option for broadening a company's product offering. Using this method, you may accommodate a wide range of customers' tastes, budgets, and special requirements. If you want to reach a wider audience and provide your customers additional ways to personalize your products, you may want to think about expanding the range of sizes, colors, materials, and packaging choices you offer.

Test New Products

It's a good idea to gauge interest in new products before fully implementing them into your online store. Soft launches and pilot programs can let you test your product with a limited audience and get valuable feedback. Make informed choices about which goods to keep, which ones to tweak, and which ones to kill off with the help of analytics tools.

Monitor and Adapt

Keep an eye on how well your new products are selling and make adjustments as appropriate. You can tell which products are doing well and which ones could use some tweaking by analyzing client responses, sales figures, and market movements. If you want to keep up with your customers and their ever-changing wants and needs, you need to conduct regular product reviews.

Expanding your product line is a great way to reach a new demographic of consumers and generate more revenue. Extending your product line requires diligent work in the areas of market research, competitive analysis, product sourcing, partnership formation, product iteration, testing, and constant monitoring and adaptation. Increase your webstore's allure and adapt to your clients' ever-changing wants and demands by stocking a wide variety of high-quality products. Let's dive into these tactics and find innovative ways to expand your company.

Managing inventory and stock levels effectively

Maintaining happy customers and a successful online store requires careful management of inventories. Meeting client needs, avoiding stockouts, and making the most of available funds are all made possible through careful inventory management. Here, we'll discuss techniques for keeping track of stock and inventory that will help you streamline operations and satisfy customers. Let's dive right into the details:

Set Optimal Stock Levels

The optimal stock level is determined by striking a balance between the two extremes of stockouts and surplus. Determine the optimal stock levels for each product by analyzing past sales data, taking into account seasonal trends, and taking into account lead times from suppliers. By doing so, you can reduce the costs associated with holding unnecessary stock while still keeping up with client demand.

Implement Inventory Tracking Systems

The ability to see current stock levels in real time and streamline inventory management operations are two major benefits of implementing an inventory tracking system. When processing orders, stock levels can be automatically updated with the help of inventory management software or integrated e-commerce platforms. Insuring precise stock counts helps you avoid overselling and disparities in stock levels by informing your purchasing selections.

Utilize Automated Reorder Systems

Automated reordering systems simplify stock replenishment and ensure it happens when it needs to. To avoid running out of stock, you can schedule automatic purchase orders to be sent as inventory reaches predetermined low points based on past sales data and estimated delivery schedules. This reduces the potential for shortages and frees up staff time by eliminating the need to calculate reorder quantities by hand.

Streamline Fulfillment Processes

Inventory management is aided by efficient fulfillment procedures. Establish efficient procedures for taking orders, packing them, and sending them out. To streamline and simplify these procedures and cut down on human error, you may want to think about integrating your webshop with order management systems or fulfillment services. Warehouse efficiency can be maximized and handling times reduced by properly planning and organizing the storage space.

Conduct Regular Stock Audits

Stock levels should be physically counted and compared to the numbers on the books on a regular basis to verify correctness. In order to ensure that your stock count is accurate, you should conduct stock audits on a regular basis. Shrinkage, broken or missing inventory, and other problems can all be uncovered in this way. Take this chance to fix inconsistencies and update your stock information.

Analyze Sales and Demand Patterns

If you track sales and demand, you may adjust your inventory and product line accordingly. Find out what items are moving the most and make sure you have enough on hand to meet client needs. You may improve your inventory management by keeping an eye on sales patterns, seasonal shifts, and product effectiveness. Learn from your customers' tastes with the use of data analytics software, and adjust your stock accordingly.

Collaborate with Suppliers and Establish Relationships

Strong supplier connections are essential for efficient inventory management. Maintaining an efficient supply chain requires constant communication with vendors, including the exchange of sales projections and talks about delivery schedules. If you're looking to reduce inventory costs and boost productivity, you can want to negotiate more accommodating terms, such more convenient payment terms or volume discounts.

Optimization of stock levels, prevention of stockouts and overstocking, and streamlining of fulfillment operations can all be attained through the use of efficient inventory management systems. Maintaining an orderly stock requires careful planning, the use of stock-tracking and automatic reordering systems, the simplification of fulfillment procedures, the execution of periodic stock audits, the examination of sales and demand patterns, and the coordination of efforts with suppliers. You may better serve your customers' needs, cut down on expenses, and keep your online store's inventory in check by following these guidelines. Together, we can improve our stock management skills by investigating these options.

Scaling your webshop to handle increased traffic and sales

Increased traffic and sales mean that your online store's infrastructure must be scaled up to maintain a positive user experience and keep up with demand. Scaling is the process of increasing your online store's capacity to process more customers, more orders, and at the same high level of performance. Here, we will discuss methods for efficiently scaling your online store to meet rising demand and sustain sustained expansion. Let's get into the details:

Optimize Your Hosting Environment

Improving your web store's hosting is a crucial first step in expanding your business. Upgrade to a more powerful and flexible hosting solution, such as a dedicated server or the cloud. Determine if your existing hosting plan can handle the influx of new customers by talking to your host about your needs. To speed up responses and cope with increased traffic, it is important to fine-tune server settings, caching methods, and database performance.

Implement Content Delivery Networks (CDNs)

Your online store's performance, especially for clients in multiple time zones, might benefit greatly from the addition of a Content Delivery Network (CDN). A content delivery network (CDN) stores and distributes the static material of your online store from numerous servers located in different locations to decrease latency and speed up page loads. Add a content delivery network (CDN) to your online store to improve loading times and uptime for customers all over the world.

Utilize Caching Techniques

By storing frequently visited data or pre-rendered pages, caching techniques assist reduce server load and improve response times. Use caching techniques such as browser caching, server-side caching, and object caching to reduce the amount of work done for each user request. Try looking at caching plugins or extensions that have been developed for your web store's platform.

Monitor and Optimize Database Performance

Maintaining webshop responsiveness as traffic grows increasingly dependent on database performance. Consider adopting database clustering or sharding to scale your database architecture and optimize your queries. To ensure effective processing of concurrent requests, it is important to regularly check database performance indicators, locate bottlenecks, and optimize queries.

Load Testing and Performance Optimization

Your online store's ability to deal with huge levels of traffic and the presence of any performance bottlenecks can be evaluated through load testing. Check how your online store reacts under hypothetically high traffic volumes. Inefficient code, slow database queries, and resource-intensive activities can all be uncovered with the use of load testing tools. Doing so will boost overall performance and make for a more pleasant user experience, even under heavy loads.

Collaborate with Web Hosting Providers

As your online store grows, don't forget to keep lines of communication open with your web host. Talk to them about what you need, how much traffic you expect, and your plans for expansion. Depending on the specifics of their hosting setup, they may be able to provide advice on how to best optimize speed, scale, and other aspects of your infrastructure. You may choose to team up with a hosting company that focuses on e-commerce to get the specialized help your web store requires.

Continuous Performance Monitoring

Your online store's performance can be monitored in real time if you set up a reliable performance monitoring system. Check data including server load, error rates, and response times. Create notifications that will inform you of any abnormalities or slowdowns. As your online store grows, it is important to monitor performance metrics and make any necessary adjustments to your infrastructure to maintain a consistent user experience.

You can make sure your online store can handle increasing traffic and sales without sacrificing efficiency if you employ efficient scaling tactics. Use Content Delivery Networks (CDNs), apply caching techniques, keep an eye on database performance, test under heavy loads, work closely with your web host, and keep performance metrics in the loop. With these methods in place, you can expand your online store to meet rising demand, provide a fantastic shopping experience, and strengthen your company's foundation for future growth. Let's dive into these tactics and find out how to make your online store more scalable.

Conclusion

In this book, we've covered a lot of ground to help you set up and manage your own online store using the powerful combination of WordPress and WooCommerce. The most important points are as follows.

- We began by gaining an appreciation for the value of using WordPress and WooCommerce to launch an online store, focusing on the advantages of both platforms and the significance of several fundamental ideas.
- We went over how to get WordPress set up, how to select a good theme, and how to modify the look and feel of your online store.
- We dove into the fundamentals of WooCommerce, investigating its capabilities and features. We then delved into the most important configuration options for your online store and provided extensive instructions for installing and setting up the WooCommerce plugin.

- We paid special attention to the creation of product categories and qualities, the efficient addition and management of products, and the efficient use of product tags for organization, guaranteeing that the product catalog on your e-commerce website is well-structured and simple to traverse.

- Managing and communicating with customers, issuing refunds and accepting returns and exchanges are all topics we discussed in detail. All of these discussions centered on how to improve customer service and reduce the time it takes to process orders.

- We covered enhancing the functionality of your webshop by adding plugins and extensions, integrating alternative payment gateways, and making use of WooCommerce themes for advanced features.

- We discussed methods for caching and optimizing your webstore's speed, safeguarding sensitive client information, and making your site accessible across a wide range of browsers and mobile devices. These guidelines contribute to a safe, quick, and faultless user experience.

- We talked about how SEO may help your online store rank higher in SERPs, get more natural clicks, and ultimately convert more browsers into buyers.

- We discussed how incorporating social media into your online store may expand your reach, build rapport with your target demographic, and eventually lead to more sales.
- To encourage sales, increase client retention, and increase repeat business, we addressed the merits of conducting promotions, offering discounts, and instituting loyalty programs.
- We underlined the value of analytics tools for monitoring customer activity and sales, analyzing this information for insights on how to improve your online store's performance.
- We discussed typical problems with an online store and how to overcome them efficiently. We also talked about the value of regularly updating your web store and maintaining backups in case something goes wrong.

Some Words of Encouragement

You have just learned everything there is to know about using WordPress and WooCommerce to set up an online store. With this knowledge in hand, you can move on with confidence as you set up your online shop.

Keep in mind that success in creating an online store comes from hard work, study, and flexibility. Recognize that online business is always changing and adapt to new methods and technologies. Maintaining a smooth shopping experience requires routinely assessing your online store's efficacy, reviewing consumer feedback, and making any necessary modifications.

You have a robust and adaptable system at your disposal with WordPress and WooCommerce. Take use of their rich ecosystem of themes, plugins, and integrations to tailor your online store to the specific demands of your brand and your customers.

You need to maintain your dedication and determination as an entrepreneur. A well-established online store is the result of hard work and a focus on the clientele. To build a loyal client base, give priority to providing superior products and services and always working to improve your marketing efforts.

Keep in mind that as an e-commerce entrepreneur, your success depends on your capacity for change, creativity, and service. Don't lose your fire, jump at new opportunities, and neglect your education. With WordPress and WooCommerce, you have the tools to turn your webstore into a successful online business.

It's time to stop procrastinating and get started making money online with WordPress and WooCommerce. Have a safe trip, and may your online store succeed beyond your wildest dreams. I hope your sales go well!

www.ingramcontent.com/pod-product-compliance
Lightning Source LLC
LaVergne TN
LVHW051345050326
832903LV00031B/3758

* 9 7 9 8 3 9 7 9 6 5 9 3 4 *